This book is dedicated to all those who want a fairer, more caring world and are prepared to do something to achieve it.

Cover design by Patricia Smart
Cover image taken from a photo of George-Lutz Rauschebart painting at the East Side Gallery. The photo was gifted to the author, photographer unknown.

German National Library bibliographic information: The German National Library lists this publication in the German National Bibliography; detailed bibliographical data can be found on the Internet at http://dnb.dnb.de

© 2019 MacLean, Christine

Production and publishing: BoD - Books on Demand, Norderstedt

ISBN 9783750405875

Contents

BERLIN, BERLIN

Understanding foreign words

BauGB	building legislation
CDU – Christlich Demokratische Union Deutschlands	Christian Democratic Union party Germany
DM - Deutschmark	West German currency before the Euro
FDJ - Freie Deutsche Jugend	Free German Youth, communist youth group
FRG	Federal Republic of Germany – West Germany
GDR	German Democratic Republic - East Germany
Hochschule der Künste	Art College
Kaderinstrukteur	Group/unit leader 'minder'
Magistrat	East Berlin equivalent of the West Berlin Senate
Palast der Republik	Palace of the Republic, lovely building which formerly stood in East Berlin
PDS – Partei des Demokratischen Sozialismus	Party of Democratic socialism
S-Bahn - Schnellbahn	fast local train which mostly travels overground
SED - Sozialistische Einheitspartei Deutschlands	the East German political party (communists)
Sekt	German 'champagne'/sparkling wine
SPD – Sozial Demokratische Partei Deutschlands	German Social Democratic party
Stasi - Staatsicherheit	East German state (secret) police
U-Bahn - Untergrundbahn	train which mostly travels underground

Where were you?

Where were you on November 9th 1989 when the Berlin Wall opened? If you are old enough to remember it, then you will almost certainly know your whereabouts. It was one of those amazing, historical events which is easily retrieved from your memory and transports you back to where you were at the time. What happened in Berlin sent ripples of change throughout the world and further reminded us of how we are all interconnected.

Images of joyful people eager to get to the parallel reality which was the West were sent around the world. Their varied emotions of apprehension, curiosity, elation and disbelief at what was taking place were palpable. The throngs seemed to be flowing through openings in the Wall which were too small to accommodate them. There was a sort of rhythm to the movement of so many separate bodies propelled in the same direction flowing like a gentle river. This river brought wave after wave of people to the unknown, uncharted waters of the West. What would they find there?

Where was I? I was there; around 15 minutes walk from Checkpoint Charlie. I had been living in West Berlin since 1979 and feeling unwell, went to bed early on November 9th. Two English friends, Adrian and Peter were visiting and when I got up on the 10th they mumbled something about watching TV and seeing people sitting on top of the Wall. They felt that something important had happened. As they didn't understand German I assumed they had been watching a film, until I opened one of the windows of my third floor flat in Yorck-strasse. The sound of many car horns assaulted my ears at first and then I noticed the smell, or rather stink, of Trabi. The smell from the East German Trabant cars with their 2 stroke engines is unmistakeable and there appeared to be hundreds of them driving along Yorckstrasse. I knew then that something significant had happened so I switched on the TV to find out that, to everyone's amazement, the borders were open.

Diary entry 10.11.89

TV and Radio full of the news and reports of people streaming across the border. Traffic on the Kudamm comes to a standstill. The place stinks like East Berlin because of the Trabis. The streets everywhere are fuller but especially the Kudamm. (Note: Kudamm is short for the Kurfürstendamm, probably the most prestigious street in West Berlin).

We had of course to go out and join in the excitement of such a momentous event. We headed down to Checkpoint Charlie and wandered along the Wall soaking up the atmosphere and vibrant mood wanting, like everyone else, to be a part of it. There were lots of people standing or sitting on the Wall, some celebrating with bottles of sekt or beer. Many had a dazed look on their faces, as though unable to believe that they were sitting on the Berlin Wall without someone trying to shoot or arrest them. The atmosphere was electric. I am sure there must have been a huge cloud filled with hope and joy floating above Berlin in those early days. Complete strangers would sometimes grab you in passing and pull you into a warm embrace wanting you to share their sheer joy.

People had already started chipping away at the Wall with chisels, screwdrivers, knives, nail files, basically anything which could be used as a tool to break off a bit of the concrete and reward them with a historical souvenir. It didn't take the capitalist mentality long to set up stands selling tools or even freshly hacked off parts of the Wall. Many parts of the west side of the Wall were very colourful having been painted or covered in graffiti for years. As days went by the paint on some pieces of the "Berlin Wall" being sold was suspiciously very fresh!

Diary entry 10.11.89

The atmosphere at Checkpoint Charlie and the Brandenburg Gate was joyful, triumphant, with people sitting on the wall and some hammering away at it.

The peaceful revolution

It's odd isn't it how we speak of the Berlin Wall falling, for it never fell. To say it fell conjures up images of it suddenly keeling over as though unable to fulfil its function any longer; it was too robust to do that. What did fall and also fail was the dictatorship which had brought the Wall into being.

The members of the East German Government didn't just wake up one morning and decide that they would allow "their" citizens freedom to travel and maybe think about opening the borders or even removing the Wall. It was the Peaceful Revolution as it is called which forced change.

On Monday October 9th 1989 after the Prayers for peace meeting, something which had been taking place since 1982 in the *Nikolaikirche* (St Nicholas church) in Leipzig, seventy thousand demonstrators took to the streets and this is considered to be the decisive date in the Peaceful Revolution. Gatherings were then held every Monday in all the large cities in East Germany and the numbers attending continued to increase. They demanded freedom of travel and the removal of the Stasi (secret police). They didn't suddenly lose their fear of the Stasi or what repercussions their actions might have; they just mastered their fears. They never knew how the Stasi would react - whether they would be beaten, arrested, tortured, imprisoned or just disappear so fear was always in the air.

Events in the GDR were preceded by unexpected developments in Hungary. On 19th August 1989, several hundred GDR citizens used the occasion of a picnic arranged by the Austrian Pan-European Union and Hungarian opposition groups to escape. On 11th September 1989 the Hungarians created an opening in the border between Hungary and Austria enabling

The peaceful revolution

GDR citizens to go to the West if they chose. The Hungarians hadn't consulted the GDR government about this move and by the end of September thousands of GDR citizens had used this exit from the East and entrance to the West. The Eastern Bloc border had thus been breached. The Berlin Wall was erected to stop the droves of people leaving for a better future in the West and you could say it came down for the same reason.

The GDR leadership didn't let these happenings faze them and carried on as usual as though everything in East Germany was wonderful. Dictators and controllers don't just give up their power it usually has to be dragged away or removed from under them. Thus the 40th anniversary of the GDR was celebrated with the usual display of killing hardware during the yearly military parade on 7th October 1989. While Erich Honecker, the Secretary General of the GDR and his cronies celebrated in the Palace of the Republic (*Palast der Republik*) after the parade, thousands of GDR citizens demonstrated their discontent outside the doors.

On November 4th 1989 what was deemed the largest post war demonstration in Germany took place as 1 million people gathered at Alexanderplatz (former East Berlin). On the evening of 9th November 1989 an announcement on GDR television declared that all citizens could travel to the West for any purpose. The GDR government could no longer deny reality and conceded that their reign (of terror) was over. The Stasi didn't however give up easily and were still attempting to carry on "business as usual" in January 1990.   .

Let's meet in Berlin

My Berlin adventure started 10 years before the Wall opened, having moved to West Berlin from Scotland in March 1979. When you look back on your life (once you have enough years behind you to do that) from an adult perspective, you notice how often fate takes a hand in your life. The reason I ended up in Berlin in the first place was through a chance meeting with someone on a ferry. Fate definitely had her eye on me.

I had been working in France for three months as an au pair and whilst on the ferry on my way home to Scotland I met Steve, an Englishman on his way back to England. Steve mentioned during the crossing that he planned to move to Germany and I asked him to keep in touch and let me know if he did. My stay in France had awakened my interest in travelling and I quite fancied going somewhere else. A few months after my return to Scotland Steve wrote me and said he was living in Berlin and if I wanted to go there we could share a flat until his girlfriend came out to join him a few months later. As I had found it difficult to settle back into life in Scotland, I took up the invitation to head to Berlin soon after receiving Steve's letter.

The long journey

Budget airlines didn't exist then and most flights were returns. If you wanted to fly one-way then you normally had to pay the price of a return and just use one leg of the journey. It seems unimaginable now in these days of cheap air travel and one-way tickets. Flying was not an option for me because of the cost involved. To get to Berlin, I took the train from Glasgow to London and after spending a couple of days in Essex with my cousins Joyce and Bobby, I headed for the ferry from Harwich to the Hook of Holland from where I took the train onwards to Berlin.

When buying my ticket at the railway station in Glasgow I remember the woman behind the counter asking me if it was for East Berlin or West Berlin, "West Berlin" said I in a panic, "I don't want to go to the East." She replied that I would have to travel through the East to get to West Berlin. It was at that point that I realised the extent of my geographic ignorance. Like many people, as I later discovered, I imagined that West Berlin was at the edge of West Germany when actually it was completely surrounded by the East and enclosed by the Berlin Wall. It was like an island but instead of being surrounded by water it was surrounded by East Germany and the communist state.

I always remember the train journey after we entered East German territory en route to West Berlin. British Rail trains had conductors to check tickets East Germany had border guards carrying guns. I had never seen a gun up close, and it was quite scary, which was of course the intention. It can be nerve wracking anyway to be alone in a foreign country where you share no common language. Communication is reduced to gestures and reading body language, particularly facial expressions. As none of the other five fellow travellers in my train compartment spoke English most of the journey was spent in silence. Fortunately we were travelling through the night, and more interested in getting some sleep between the interruptions to check our documentation than having a conversation.

The soldier looked confused when handed my passport. He then gave me one of those intimidating looks, often the demeanour of those wearing a uniform. A lot of civil servants or uniformed personnel whom I encountered in Germany seemed to have been chosen for their resemblance to guard dogs as they often had a fierce exterior and snapping manner. I soon learned that if you snapped back at them they tended to jump backwards as they weren't used to that.

The train travelled through East Germany for about two or three hours in order to get to West Berlin. Driving to West Berlin from West Germany took about the same amount of time or even longer, depending on which route was used but border delays happened frequently if the East Germans decided to be awkward.

You could be held up at the start of the transit route as it was called to have your car searched. A car search wasn't just merely a rummage through your bags and suitcases. It could involve having to remove the back seat or other structures. They were searching for people attempting to escape. The underside of the vehicle would also be checked to see if anyone was prepared to risk their life to escape by hiding under the vehicle. For this they used a mirror mounted horizontally on small wheels which they pushed under the car.

You could be delayed en route and sit in a "traffic jam" for ages although nothing visible appeared to be causing it. If that happened you were expected to stay in your car.

It was strictly forbidden to stop and get out of your car on the transit route. You were literally at the mercy of the East German Border Guards and they knew it. You needed of course to have proper documentation to be able to travel through the "corridor" as the route between West Berlin and West Germany was also named and aptly so. You were timed at the border control when you left and again when you arrived at the other end. This was to ensure that you didn't stop and try to smuggle someone out, go off route, or meet up with someone from the East. If the time it took you to drive through the corridor didn't add up to their satisfaction you could find yourself in a lot of trouble.

All entrance and exit roads off the transit route were under strict surveillance. The Border Guards and their cars were so well concealed at these points that you didn't notice them. Their presence only became obvious to anyone who dared go off route because they perhaps desperately needed to pee. Everyone who travelled the corridor regularly knew that there would be no such thing as a toilet break so either you had to cross your legs tightly for a few hours or pee into a bottle in the moving car (not so difficult for men but quite a trial for women).

The long journey

If your luck was out you could be held up at the transit border for hours without reason. It was just pure intimidation. It could happen that a border guard spent twenty minutes alternately staring you in the face and then looking at your documentation to decide whether you were really the person you claimed to be. The angrier this treatment made you and especially if you let your anger show or even worse, dared to say something, the longer they kept you waiting. If your passport photo was old, or of poor quality then they could keep you waiting for hours or in the worst case, not let you through at all. After all, to the East Germans you were from the wicked, debauched capitalist West and they probably relished the opportunity to hold power over you, however briefly.

Andrew's border ordeal

I was in my mid-20s and had been assigned a posting attached to the British Forces Education Service in Western Germany. This was at a time about 30 years after Germany's defeat in the Second World War, when the four main allies in Europe - the United States, Great Britain, the Soviet Union, and France – were still engaged in the joint occupation of the German state, with the original understanding that the partitioned country, East and West would eventually be reunified.

I fell instantly head over heels in love with Germany – its cuisine, its work-hard-play-hard culture, the varied scenery from the smoggy industrial Ruhr to the fresh air and snow clad mountains topped in the springtime with myriad Alpine flowers. From my mid-teens, when I chose the German language as a specialist subject in school, I had become enamoured with all things German, supported by many stories from my father who had been a soldier in Cologne during the Second World War and from newspaper reports of cold-war events. At the earliest opportunity after my arrival, I decided not to spend much time associating with people in the British community and instead, to make friends in the German one. I did not want to live out the East/West Division by only associating with my own nationality; we would never bring down die Mauer (the Wall) if we did not build Brücken (bridges.)

Of my many and varied work projects, one took me regularly to Berlin. I lived in what was then the West and so had the excitement of driving through the West/East corridor with all that that entailed; there were severe restrictions on the movement of East German citizens from East to West. For we

Andrew's border ordeal

Westerners, especially those connected to the British military and governments, the border could be crossed legally only through a limited number of air, road, rail and river routes. I always chose to drive via the border point at Helmstedt, and the Marienborn crossing point, checkpoint codenamed Alpha, then skirting Magdeburg in East Germany, entering East Berlin, under Russian control, via the Potsdam crossing point, known as Checkpoint Bravo. Whichever route and means you took each had its own complications. At Marienborn, you signed in by presenting a passport through a small slot in a tiny cupboard-like room at the Russian check-in point; you had no way of seeing who stood or sat behind it though I was always convinced the Russians could easily see me. Even one comma mismatching on documents was enough for you to be denied access.

Papers presented, you were required to immediately return to your car by presenting the papers again to a Russian or was it an East German guard for final checking and a further salute. The look of misery on some of these young soldiers' faces triggered in me a deep sense of sadness. On misty mornings it was like something out of a spy movie. But it did add to the mystery and excitement.

The return journey required me to check in at the American crossing point, codenamed Bravo, an altogether different kettle of fish, a huge, spacious room with large posters giving advice and warnings. Then an American official came and gave us, in hurried sharp fashion, a briefing about how we were to proceed through the corridor. We were given a set amount of time to make the journey and given an ETA (Estimated Time of

Andrew's border ordeal

Arrival.) If this time had elapsed and we had not arrived at our destination, then all manner of searches would be undertaken until we were found. We were warned that if we stopped our car for any reason, eg to stop for a pee, and were arrested by East German or Russian soldiers, the Russians being in control of Eastern Germany, then we should not speak, we should only ask for the most senior Russian Officer and then wait till either the next British, French, or American search convoy passed and took us away. Other than that, road crossings were fairly straightforward but slow because of these extensive border formalities and inspections. But it was clear drivers were required to stay on designated transit routes across East Germany.

On one such occasion returning from Berlin, I was aware that the briefing by the American soldier was incredibly detailed and as always, in my experience, rushed. Had I not known previously what the briefing was about I would have been hard pressed to remember it. On this notable occasion I was aware that the only others being briefed with me were a young American soldier and his wife. It was blindingly obvious that both were finding it difficult to understand the briefing information and they looked intimidated and shell shocked. In time we set off in our respective cars. I remember as I exited the car to present my papers to the Russians that I had logged the looks of terror in my fellow American travellers' faces and had made a mental note that, as far as possible, I would travel the Autobahn slightly slower, within permitted limits, until they caught up with me; after all, we had been briefed to look out for each other along the way so that should we see the other in trouble we could report it at the next border crossing point. We had been briefed never to get out of our car during the travel from East to West or vice versa, along the corridor.

After about an hour's drive I had a gnawing sense of dread in my gut; my American travellers had not overtaken me and were nowhere to be seen behind. I couldn't travel more slowly, at least not legally. Had they failed at the first hurdle with the checking-in with the Russians? After about twenty minutes worrying about what I should do, I did what we had been briefed not to do – stop at the next layby which allowed me full view of the autobahn so I could look out for my "friends." I did not get out of the car!

Within seconds my car was surrounded by Russian soldiers and to this day I know not from whence they "emerged" - presumably the ditch. I did as I was told and wound down my window a fraction in order to say, "Ich möchte bitte mit einem hochrangigen russischen Offizier sprechen," "I want to speak to a senior Russian officer." No matter the reply from the Russians my instructions were to say only that one sentence which I had to repeat many times for it seemed they either had no Senior Russian Officer present or had no intention of finding him. This charade continued for several hours by which time I was well past the ETA at the next border crossing-point and had been so distracted it would have been impossible for me to notice if my friends had caught up.

In time, a senior Russian officer appeared; I was suddenly allowed to go and continued on my journey, feeling relieved but also disappointed that I had failed in my mission to be a supportive ally. I reached the Marienborn crossing feeling overwhelmingly glad to have arrived back on western soil; but the real drama was only just about to begin.

The British military knew I was late in arriving by hours and so, without any attempt at conversation, I was frog marched into a small dingy room with a desk and chair and a light bulb overhead. "I'm sure it will swing," I thought to myself whilst wondering what was going to happen next. This wondering was short lived when a rough sergeant major type official landed me a slap on the face and growled out the question, "Did you not get a briefing and were you not told what to do in the event you had a breakdown?" My efforts to explain that I had not had a breakdown and that I had only wanted to help an ally fell on deaf and stupid, "I'm only carrying out my orders," ears. I became increasingly concerned at successive blows to my body in places where marks would not be made, and where I was left in no doubt a blow had landed. I wondered how long it would go on. Who had given these orders? Was everyone who defaulted treated this way? Why could they not respond to a reasoned tone and calm, rational explanation?

The question as to why I didn't associate with Brits and socialised instead mainly with Germans was asked by 'the voice'. (I thought to myself, "Well if you know that much about whom I associate with then you should know that my socialising carries no risk to cold war connections between East and West.") But the more reasonable I became, the worse the nightmare. Hours later, when I heard the voice let me go and instruct me "to never do it again," I noticed, the light bulb was swinging, but only from the energy, the draught from the flying fists.

Andrew's border ordeal

I thought that was the end of that but in later years both in Germany and in London, I became the subject of enquiry several times over; it seemed that once a suspect, always a suspect. It left me suspicious of our secret service and whilst I understand the need to carry out orders, the low level of intelligence behind the reasoning and the orders, questions, and the "you're guilty until we find out otherwise" attitude is something I will never understand. I have forgiven, but I will not forget.

I ought to have felt safe arriving at a British military compound on the East-West border and sure of a warm welcome but instead I was treated like a criminal, shouted at and harangued.

Andrew

The cold of Prussia

Christine's story

On March 21st 1979 after the long journey from my starting point in Glasgow, I finally arrived in West Berlin at the Zoo train station, (Zoologischer Garten). It was around 6am and still quite dark. My first memory after arrival is of walking through the dingy underground tunnel leading from the station, ascending the steps at the other end and emerging onto Hardenbergstrasse to, what was for me, a very alien world.

The piles of snow at the side of the road bore witness to a long white winter and it was bitterly cold. I had never encountered such cold in Scotland. There seems to be a strange notion that Scotland is freezing cold in winter and we have lots of snow which just isn't true. In Berlin winters it wasn't unusual for the temperature to drop as low as -30°C, as I soon discovered. However, unlike Scotland the cold in Berlin is a dry cold which is far preferable to the damp cold in Scotland which seems to make even your bones shiver.

Fortunately I had the advantage of being met at the station by Steve. Although I had only met him fleetingly, it gave me an easier start in Berlin than if I hadn't known a soul. At that time Steve was renting part of an apartment in Schlüterstrasse in the Charlottenburg district which was in the British sector. Part of an apartment sounds a bit weird and it certainly was weird to me but the landlady had divided her apartment and Steve was renting what we would probably call two rooms, a makeshift kitchen and bathroom within the apartment. That was where I spent the first three months of my new life in West Berlin, sharing Steve's half of a half apartment.

Love at first Light

I fell in love with Berlin when I saw it in the light of day. I can't explain it but I just felt at home. I loved the wide streets and broad pavements which gave the feeling you had room to expand, could spread your wings, open out and be whatever you wanted.

Although a big city, there was lots of greenery as many streets were graced by beautiful trees and throughout Berlin there were many parks. The old apartment buildings were beautiful and although some ugly modern buildings had been erected between rows of elegant flats because the original building was perhaps destroyed in the war, this didn't detract from the grand overall effect. Obviously there were some districts which were more attractive than others but the city in its entirety still impressed. West Berlin was divided into districts each one being well supplied with shops removing the need to go to the centre. This meant you got to know your neighbours quicker as it was inevitable you would meet whilst food shopping which you could do on foot.

I really took to the German people and the way of life in Berlin. Noticing the number of pubs and chemists made me initially wonder if this was a nation of drunken hypochondriacs. I had never seen so many chemists anywhere else. Some chemists sold homeopathic remedies along with pharmaceuticals and there were health food shops selling health supplements, organic cosmetics and toiletries long before they became fashionable elsewhere.

Most Germans I met often asked two questions: How old are you? and How many people live in your home town? I found the second question really odd because first of all that isn't something I or most people I know are even interested in but it seems that a German will judge the size of your town or city by the number of inhabitants. With that they might also suss you out as a townie or country bumpkin. How quaint I thought! You just never stop learning and having the chance to view things from another perspective.

On entering small shops such as bakers it was common for everyone to say good morning or good afternoon. I am not sure if it was addressed solely at the assistants or at the waiting customers as well but it was a nice touch. This was a contrast to the often gruff manner of true Berliners. They even have a name for it "Berliner Schnauze" (Berlin snout)! It took a bit of getting used to but if you gave as good as you got then that was usually respected.

As my accommodation for a few months was sorted the next priority was to find employment. With little knowledge of German, I found my first job as an office worker in one of the British Army stores in Spandau.

A native English speaker in Berlin in the late 70s and 80s easily found work if English was a requirement. Germans didn't speak English very well in those days, (since then the use of computers has promoted the universal learning of the English language). It was a pretty boring typing job but it was a start. The only downside for me was travelling from Charlottenburg to Spandau every day for a 7am start, a journey which took over an hour. There isn't much pleasure in leaving the house at 5.30am on cold, dark mornings. Travelling by underground most of the way to work meant that it took me months to figure out where I was when above ground until I started going about by bus or on foot. It was a bit like joining up the dots but in this case the dots were the underground stations and the world above them. After a year I quit that boring job and flew to Greece for adventure on the high seas returning to Berlin a few months later.

West Berlin, probably in common with most big cities, was a transient city where people came and went. Some stayed a few months others several years before either returning to their roots or moving elsewhere.

As under Allied Law (passed after the Second World War) it was forbidden for West Berlin to have its own army it made the city very attractive for those West Germans who disagreed with conscription. A number of them moved to West Berlin to avoid having to serve in the West German army taking advantage of West Berlin's special status under Allied control. Despite this special status however, some of those opposed to serving in the army were still arrested and jailed by the Berlin Police.

In a new country there were of course new customs to learn; if you were religious then you paid a church tax which was deducted from your salary every month; when your birthday was celebrated you were the one who bought the cake; December 6th was called *Nikolaus* an important date for children when they received a small gift or sweets; Christmas was celebrated on December 24th when families got together in the evening to have their Christmas meal and the Christmas tree was only put up on December 24th.

Love at first Light

In December I had the delight of discovering the wonderful Christmas markets with their beckoning lights twinkling in the winter darkness which fell so early. The memory of my first visit to a Christmas market is very vivid and I can clearly recall; the sound of happy voices enjoying themselves; the smell and taste of Glühwein, the hot liquid spreading through your chilled body causing an instant internal glow and the seasonal aromas of oranges and spices such as nutmeg and cinnamon wafting enticingly, invitingly in the air so cold, your breath was visible as it left you. Heavenly.

New Year in Berlin was a fun event with fireworks lighting up the sky at midnight, happy people on the streets on their way to parties or clubs and pubs. My memories of New Year in Scotland were nothing like that. For the first time, I really enjoyed New Year's Eve.

Strange new things

For me Berlin was definitely a culture shock but in the most interesting, exciting way. It was so different from East Kilbride, the small, modern new town I had just left in Scotland. If you can't find yourself in Berlin then I don't think you ever will. Nobody seemed to bat an eyelid at how you were dressed or even undressed, nor did they care who or how you wanted to be. In most parts of Scotland if you dressed differently from the masses then your mother was likely to make the comment, "You're not going out like that are you, what will the neighbours think?" It seemed in Berlin nobody gave a damn what the neighbours thought. Everything was possible and everyone was accepted as they were. It was very liberating. Berlin isn't of course representative of the rest of Germany in the same way that Glasgow isn't representative of the whole of Scotland. Berlin is just Berlin.

The absence of men wearing suits and ties was interesting. Both the men and women were smartly dressed for work but their attire was much more relaxed and casual.

I take great pleasure in visiting different countries, discovering new things and learning about other customs. Some of these things can be good, bad or indifferent, depending on your viewpoint. One of the first strange things, at least for me, I experienced in Berlin was when I went to the public swimming pool.

On entering the pool area after changing into my swimming costume, I glanced at a man swimming in the pool and felt that something wasn't right but it took a few moments for my brain to realise that he was completely naked apart from a swimming cap. I was shocked that he was in the nude and recall thinking to myself, "These Germans have some funny ideas. Why on earth would someone be naked but wear a swimming cap?" Nobody had told me that it was the nude bathing session but it still didn't make any sense to me that you bared your bum but covered your head. Nude bathing in public places in Scotland is unheard of and if you tried it you would probably get arrested.

The second strange experience along similar lines took place in a spa which is still there to this day. It's on the 4th floor of a building near the Zoo and is called Thermen. It's a great setup with swimming pools (one which allows you to swim outside), saunas, steam rooms, café etc where you can spend an hour or two or the entire day.

People have no inhibitions whatsoever about sitting in the sauna in the nude or walking about the complex with a loose bathing robe letting it all hang out. You certainly wouldn't have that experience in Scotland in a spa complex.

On my first visit there, I was having a public shower. I hadn't chosen to shower in public but there were no cubicles or shower curtains. I was washing myself with a bar of 'Pears' soap which if you have never seen it, is unusual, because it's translucent. The guy showering next to me was a very tall Black American and was really taken with my soap, so there we were both stark naked, complete strangers, discussing a bar of soap. Now how's that for something different?

It's just what you are used to I suppose and the Germans are quite relaxed about nudity, unlike the British. Offer a massage to the average German for example and they have stripped off and are lying on the massage table before you can blink whereas if you make the same offer to the average Brit you are likely to be asked, "Do I have to take my clothes off?" As a qualified massage therapist, I have actually been asked that question by an Englishman.

Everyone should travel abroad when they are young and I mean travel, not go on some package tour to the sun to eat the same food you get back home, in restaurants owned by someone from your home country. That isn't travelling. To really travel you need to go off the beaten track, mix with the local people, sample their food and explore their culture.

In the 80s and 90s travelling within Europe was still interesting, that was before the global junk food purveyors destroyed real food and global cheap clothes shops created an almost clone society. We had much more freedom; that was before the omnipresent Orwellian surveillance systems and before we were herded like cattle through airports using the excuse of security to degrade us. Now you need to travel much further afield to experience really different cultures and cuisines as Europe has become, in many instances, too similar and thus, for me, a bit boring.

The opening hours of shops in Berlin took a bit of getting used to. In Scotland Saturday was and in some ways still is the main shopping day. It is a day when people meet up with others, go shopping with their family and catch up with things they couldn't get done during the working week.

In Berlin at that time the shops closed at 2pm on Saturdays except for the first Saturday in the month which was referred to as long Saturday because the department stores and supermarkets (but not small independent shops) stayed open until 4pm. Bleary-eyed, hungover people trying to shop at the last minute on Saturdays before the shops closed until Monday was a fairly common sight. The main train station was the only option for emergency supplies outwith these trading hours. Turkish grocers were always a bit more relaxed about their closing times and often remained open until 3 or 4pm.

The opening hours of shops in Berlin, including Saturday, have now changed drastically and most stay open until 8pm, some supermarkets until 10pm or later. The majority of shops in Berlin still don't open on a Sunday however, unless they are considered a tourist shop. I must admit I like that as it makes Sundays much quieter and more restful than the rest of the week. That's something which is now rare in the average city.

For better or worse

When you go abroad, especially for the first time, you tend to compare all aspects of your new life to the life you knew back home. You find out that some things are better and some perhaps less so. The public transport system in Scotland has always been a bit of a joke but here in Berlin I was pleasantly surprised to discover that the buses and trains arrived on time and everything ran smoothly. I also noticed that it wasn't just poor people who couldn't afford a car who used the public transport system. In Berlin you didn't need to have a car precisely because the public transport system was so good.

The ticketing system was well thought out too. You could buy one ticket which was valid on the bus, U-bahn (underground) and S-bahn (local fast train) so you could change from one to the other easily without having to buy separate tickets. That made a lot of sense to me. So Berlin for me really highlighted how many things in Scotland just weren't working very well. Sadly the public transport system in Berlin and Germany is no longer as efficient or reliable but still not as bad as in many parts of Scotland where the majority of the transport system is in private ownership and where the mantra is "profit before people."

There were only two U-Bahn lines in East Berlin, Pankow-Thälmannplatz/Mohrenstrasse and Alexanderplatz-Tierpark. What they did have in the East however was an extensive tram system whereas there were no trams in the West. Travelling on the tram is definitely my preferred method of public transport.

For better or worse

An efficient public transport system makes life in general much easier. Knowing that the bus or train will arrive on time means that you can get to the stop at the same time every day and your day can start in a relaxed manner.

In Scotland, you live in hope that a bus will arrive. You always need an alternative plan and usually you leave home earlier than necessary just in case the bus or train doesn't turn up at all or to allow for delays. You could understandably get the impression that in Scotland delays are part of the normal schedule. If the bus doesn't turn up at all then you may be stranded if you live in a rural area, have to find money for a taxi or just walk. That's the kind of stress you don't have when public transport systems are dependable.

What I did miss in Berlin however with regard to public transport, was the orderly queuing system we have in Scotland. It seemed as though it was every man and woman for themselves in Berlin. We used to joke about the elderly ladies being the ones to watch out for when queuing for a bus as they had a knack of elbowing you in the ribs or walloping you on the legs with their umbrellas or walking sticks if they thought you were getting in front of them. That behaviour surprised me as my overall impression of the Germans was that they tended to be orderly and obedient.

There were (and still are) no barriers at the entrance to train stations so random checks on tickets were made by controllers clad in blue uniforms and blue hats. We used to call them Bluebottles. Several of them would get into a carriage all entering by different doors so that nobody could dive out. The old underground trains had three doors and a controller would stand at each of the doors blocking all chances of escape. Sometimes they were waiting on the platform for people to alight and caught fare dodgers that way.

Today the controllers are all dressed like the rest of the public so not easy to spot. They show no mercy if you don't have a ticket and not having cash won't shake them off as they are set up to take card payments. If you are resident in Berlin and get caught a few times you end up in court. One of their favoured places to wait these days is just before and also at Schönefeld airport as the Berlin travel network is divided into zones for pricing and at the stop before Schönefeld it enters zone C. It is a great trap for tourists because either they knowingly don't pay for zone C as most of them will be spending their time in Zones A and B or they are just clueless. Either way it is an expensive mistake and pleading ignorance because you are a foreigner won't get you off the hook. Germans are sticklers for their rules and regulations! If you have neither cash nor a credit card they will demand your passport details.

The U-Bahn and S-Bahn stations have a central platform with tracks to the right and left of it or tracks in the middle and platforms at either side. A small oblong office with a glass viewing area on both sides was situated about the middle of the platform. These were used by the train controller or "get in don't get in commanders" as we Brits called them. The staff told you to get into the train which had just pulled in to the station (we Brits thought that it was pretty obvious that when a train arrived you would get into it and that it wasn't something you needed to be told to do. Did you really need to pay someone to do this?) When the doors were about to close the train controller would announce the stay back command over the tannoy system. Now, not everyone obeyed the command to stay back and many made a run for it to get onto the train at the last minute before the doors closed with a wince inducing thump. This caused some of these controllers to get really annoyed so they then shouted, "Staaaay back!" into their microphones, usually in a very irate tone. They obviously weren't very happy about their command being disobeyed. These controllers no longer exist, the task having been given to the train drivers.

One mode of transport I really took to in Berlin was going about on a bike. I hadn't been on a bike since childhood and it was great to have the freedom of cycling around which took you further than you could perhaps walk whilst you were still out in the fresh air and it was free. The thing that makes cycling in Berlin such fun is the designated bike lanes which you find everywhere from streets in outlying areas to the main shopping streets. I never saw a cyclist in any kind of lycra gear or even wearing a helmet. People just wore their everyday clothes and then got on their bikes. It reminded me of seeing films shot in the 1950s in Britain where people did exactly the same. Cycling in Scotland often means taking your life in your hands. There are very few designated cycling lanes and the mentality of most drivers is to treat cyclists like a pain in the neck. Cyclists in Scotland are also often expected to share a pavement with pedestrians; something which isn't ideal for either party.

Police State

One thing I found strange was living in a police state where it was a legal requirement for every resident, to register at their local Residents Registration office. Every time you move home in Germany you have to register your new address with the authorities.

My first residence permit entitled me to stay for a few months and after renewing it a couple of times I could then remain in Germany indefinitely. I applied for my first permit very soon after arriving. It was really helpful having the advice of Steve who had been there that little bit longer and who had received tips and advice from other foreigners on how to navigate the sea of German bureaucracy.

On the evening before my visit to the Foreign Police in Putkamerstrasse, Kreuzberg to have my photo taken and apply for my permit, Steve was giving me a few tips. "Stay serious and don't try to make jokes with the police or staff. The Germans separate work and leisure time very clearly so they don't laugh at work, especially not the civil servants, that is reserved for life outside work," he said. "It isn't like back home where people laugh when they hear or see something funny regardless of where they are, so you need to be aware of that," he said seriously. "Gosh, can that really be true?" I thought. I could see myself having difficulty with that.

"By the way, he added, "don't forget you will have to show your right ear tomorrow" "My right ear I thought, while an instinctive reflexive action immediately sent my hand to my right ear in a protective gesture. "Why on earth do I have to show my right ear, and why only the right ear? Did the Germans use your ear for identification?" "What do you mean I have to show my right ear Steve?" I asked anxiously? "Do they examine it or worse, take an earprint instead of a fingerprint?" Steve laughed, "No, no they don't examine your ear. They want you to turn your head slightly to the left so that part of your right ear is in the photo, don't ask me why. Turning your head slightly gives them a different profile maybe. It isn't like back home where you look straight into the camera for your passport photo (we don't have identity cards in the UK and not everyone has a passport)". "Oh" I said, relieved that my ear wasn't going to be examined but simply put in the picture. I still found it a bit strange. Anyway, off I went the next day, behaving seriously with an appropriate look on my face and flaunted my right ear for what was probably its first photo.

I had always found Steve's statement about the Germans not laughing at work difficult to believe. It was also more the true Berliners who were meant here, as Germans from other parts of Germany would hasten to emphasise. A number of years later however, I was working in a German call centre and whilst chatting on the phone one day I started laughing. The entire room of around thirty German colleagues stopped what they were doing, turned and stared at me. "So I thought, maybe Steve wasn't so wrong after all!"

The UK may not appear a police state but it is just more devious about how it watches you. There are probably more surveillance cameras in the UK than in any other country in the world. You would be a fool to think that our state police are any less ruthless than in any other country in fact the behaviour of the British Secret Service compared to a criminal organisation in a recent news article. The British

Police State

Government will stop at nothing to get what it wants, just look at the history of the British Empire. The British flag, in many former colonies is called "the Butcher's apron."

For an insight into some of the atrocities committed by the British Empire in one of its colonies, India, I can recommend the book *Inglorious Empire*, by Shashi Tharoor.

Life is good

Living in Berlin, in contrast to the life I had known in Scotland was much easier in many ways. One plus point was the ease of travel to foreign countries where you could just get into a train or a bus and end up in another country. From an island like the UK that was impossible as you either had to sail or fly over a large body of water first which of course greatly added to the expense.

The car share service *Mitfahrgelegenheit,* was a great discovery. You could get a lift to and from Berlin or anywhere else in Germany and beyond, for very little money. This was a brilliant idea which enabled drivers to cover some or all of their costs by taking paying passengers.

It was all well organised and safe, as drivers and passengers registered with an agency which arranged lifts and matched up both parties with times and destinations. There was a limit to how much a driver could charge passengers. This was probably down to how much the petrol cost as the more passengers a driver took the cheaper it became for each one.

Although Berlin enchanted me from day one, there were obviously things I missed from home such as the British sense of humour. I met up with several other Brits through time and we all came to the conclusion that the German sense of humour was nothing like our own and that Germans tended to take offence if you tried to crack jokes with and about them. Much of British humour is about making fun of yourself and being able to take a joke but we Brits discovered that didn't go down well with the majority of Germans we met. It was also extremely annoying for native English speakers that films were dubbed into German, especially if the film was a comedy as the translation usually killed off any hint of humour.

It was in Berlin however that I discovered "Dinner for One." This, if you have never heard of it, is an English comedy starring Freddie Frinton which has become an institution in Germany as it is shown on TV every New Year's Eve and on several channels. It was made in 1963 and has been aired on German TV for over 40 years. As far as I am aware, it has never been shown on British TV and was completely unknown to me prior to living in Germany. One of the lines in it, "the same procedure as last year" is now firmly embedded in the German language.

It seemed as though everything in Berlin was more affordable than back home. This was especially the case when shopping at the many markets. One of my favourite haunts was the Turkish outdoor markets which sold anything from clothes to a cucumber much cheaper than in most shops. I realised fairly quickly that you could actually have a life in Berlin rather than just existing in survival mode.

The cost of living in Britain is high and has been for years. The Highlands of Scotland in particular is a very expensive place to live yet employees are often paid way below those in the south of England or other parts of the UK in general, sometimes for doing the same job with the same company.

One great advantage of my improved living standard in Berlin was that eating out and exploring the various pubs, cafés and music venues was so affordable. In Berlin I discovered a whole new world where people went into pubs to socialise, not just to get drunk and that food was served in most pubs. A common pastime I quickly adopted was meeting friends for breakfast at any time of day.

The pubs also tended to be lighter and brighter and without a beer sodden carpet! I detested Scottish pubs which usually had a carpet on the floor which had so much beer spilt on it that the stench of stale beer met you at the door. Why on earth would you put a carpet on the floor of a pub where the customers wanted their beer glasses filled to the brim so that even before they got drunk, pints of it had already soaked into the carpet?

There was also none of the "round buying" which I found so senseless in Scotland, especially for someone who didn't drink alcohol. Each member of a group in turn would buy a "round" of drinks for all. It often led to people drinking more than they wanted as they felt pressure was put on them to drink at the same pace as the fastest drinker among them. The German custom of buying your own drink seemed a much more relaxed, mature system.

It was and is usual in cafés or bars in Berlin to pay your bill before you leave, the waiter or waitress having kept a running tab for you. This brought the thought to mind that the Germans must be pretty honest for such a system to be successful. The few exceptions to this custom which I came across were in places frequented by lots of Brits, especially if they were part of the military!

Life is good

There are lots of excellent snack bars (*Imbiss)* in Berlin and the quality and freshness of the street food in most of these is superior to what is served in many restaurants in the UK. One of the best and now (thanks to social media) most well-known is *Mustafas* on Mehringdamm. It has become so popular that the minimum waiting time for a delicious Döner whether chicken or vegetarian is probably around one hour.

Food for the soul

Berlin opened up for me a feast of culinary delights which I was only too willing to partake of. Good quality, tasty food doesn't just fill your stomach it nourishes your soul.

The typical German fare was not for me though as it tended to centre round dead flesh. The German baked goods however, particularly the rye and sourdough bread were definitely to my liking. I would seek out different bakers throughout the city on a regular basis to try their products. My preference for meals was to go to one of the Arabic, Turkish, Greek or Indian restaurants.

Many districts had an indoor market, with a seemingly unending variety of quality foods and on every day of the week except Sunday you could find an outdoor market somewhere to visit. Some stands would be piled high with a variety of fruit and vegetables showing their best colours, other stands sold socks, shoes, clothes, tea, snacks etc. (On Sundays, if you were a market junkie, you could visit the flea markets). The outdoor markets were there regardless of the weather. The goods were far cheaper than in most shops and near the end of the day, especially on Saturdays when there were no markets the next day, fresh food was almost given away.

My favourite outdoor market was and still is the Turkish one at the Maybachufer. Fabrics, one of my passions, were so cheap that I had to limit my purchases or I would have been forced to move home because of lack of space. Most of the vendors were regular stallholders, but some entrepreneurs rented a stall for a week or two to sell treasures brought back from a trip to India, Thailand or Africa, the proceeds of their sales buying their next ticket to exotica.

Food for the soul

I always admired the patience of the vendors as they set up their stands, arranged the display of their goods and then at close of day packed what was left and dismantled everything.

The smells and sounds, the whole atmosphere which you absorb whilst shopping at these markets is a sensory experience which can never be had in a sterile supermarket or impersonal shopping mall filled with the same shops selling the same stuff, regardless of where in the world it is located.

Not so nice

One of the least pleasing things in Berlin which I discovered however was dog shit! It was a huge problem and sometimes so bad that you felt you had to dance around the piles like a child playing a game where the aim was to avoid walking on cracks in the paving or similar.

Once you lived there for a while you seemed to develop a kind of radar in your feet, a kind of unconscious scanning technique of the way ahead which usually enabled you to avoid the many unpleasant piles of brown stuff on the pavements. You could always spot the tourists as they were the ones admiring the buildings or looking up at the skyline and then went splat as they stepped into a pile of dog shit. The only time I felt the squelch was on a visit to Berlin a few years after I had left. My radar system, once so finely honed, had failed due to lack of use.

Keeping them apart

People in Germany didn't seem to be separated into the same hierarchy that I knew from back home. The class system in the UK is a perversity and in Scotland there is religious segregation in state schools. How can this possibly improve our acceptance of others? It breeds the belief in our formative years that there is somehow a difference between us and creates unnatural divisions where there should be none.

I spent the first eight years of my life in a small village called Ardersier in the Highlands of Scotland. All the children went to the only village school, so there was no religious segregation. In my ninth year we moved to East Kilbride at that time a new town near Glasgow. The whole family hated East Kilbride and as soon as we were adults, each of us headed off abroad or anywhere but East Kilbride. It was when I got to East Kilbride that I found out about this religious segregation which up to that point was a completely alien concept to me and had nothing to do with my young age.

I couldn't understand how neighbours went to a different school just because they were in a different church. For the first time I heard the words Catholics and Protestants and their short forms Cathies and Proddies, usually used as insults, especially among supporters of the two main football teams in Scotland. In the Central Belt (Glasgow, Edinburgh) in particular potential employees were selected for a job using the main criteria of whether they went to a Catholic or Protestant school. This was certainly very common up until the 80s and the sad reflection on our society is that it was condoned.

Busting a myth

Somehow the belief has been accepted as fact that the Germans are efficient but that in my opinion is a myth. They are very precise and exact and this is definitely a great characteristic to have when dealing with machines and inanimate objects but when it comes to dealing with people the officials, in particular, were often very rigid. Germans are sticklers for rules and regulations which at times can express itself as a lack of humanity. Flexibility isn't the first word which springs to mind when describing the Germans in general.

One example of this lack of flexibility which I observed was when sitting in an almost empty cinema one time and two minutes before the start of the film a German asked the person in front of me to move because he was sitting in his seat! He could have chosen from any number of empty seats but no he was insistent on having that one.

As an example of modern day German **in**efficiency you just have to look at the new airport being built at Schönefeld which is years overdue, is a permanent work in progress and some of the infrastructure is already out of date before it is even completed. The cause for this, which for the Germans is a hugely embarrassing mess, is said to be gross inefficiency, incompetence and some suspect even corruption.

First visit to East Berlin

Shortly after my arrival in Berlin Steve suggested we cross over to the East side. West Berlin was exotic and different enough for me so what was the East going to be like, I thought. I had been taught nothing about German history (I wasn't taught much Scottish history either!) in school and knew very little about the Wall. However, the anxiety I felt when the woman at the ticket desk in Glasgow told me I would have to travel through the East to get to West Berlin surely meant that I had picked up something about communism and the Wall somewhere along the way.

One morning at the beginning of April, Steve and I left the American sector and crossed the border at Checkpoint Charlie on foot. This was probably when I became fully cognisant of the Wall and got a feel for what it must have meant to those enclosed within it. Not being a German obviously meant that my feelings about the Berlin Wall weren't perhaps so emotionally charged as a German's but that didn't mean that this symbol of the "Cold War" left me completely cold because I became increasingly aware of the personal suffering of many Germans I met.

Have you ever visited someone in jail? I have and I clearly remember the chill which ran down my spine as each door I went through, of which there were several, was locked behind me. My imagination ran wild as I feared being mistaken for a prisoner and not getting back out when visiting time was over. Going through the border that day brought up the same wild imaginings and fears.

First visit to East Berlin

The East German Border Guards may not have had a bunch of keys and there may not have been as many doors closing behind you but the feeling of powerlessness was similar.

The layout of the borders was often designed so that the way through either on foot or by car was neither straight nor direct. That was obviously to deter anyone from making a run for it or driving straight at it in an attempt to escape. It was much more difficult to get up speed if you had to negotiate corners and on foot there were often several unmarked doors which you had to pass through, all of which tended to be painted the uniform GDR grey.

Up to that point I had mainly spent my time in the Charlottenburg district where I wasn't faced with the Wall in front of my window or even round the corner. When you were out and about exploring West Berlin and maybe went up a street to find the Wall blocking your way then that of course brought the whole thing closer to home. For someone in West Berlin it may have seemed a nuisance to backtrack and take another route but at least we could change direction and it wasn't that much of an inconvenience. Once you lived in an area for a while you got to know the routes you could take without being blocked by the Wall at some point so it went out of your mind. Imagine your counterpart on the other side of the Wall. Firstly they would not have been permitted to get within touching distance of the Wall and fear would have kept them much further back than that anyway.

One example of bizarre situations in the East was Brehmestrasse in the Pankow district, where there was a barbed wire fence and barrier in the middle of the street. This street was directly on an S-Bahn line (above ground) leading to Frohnau in the West. The residents of the flats couldn't open the windows on the west-facing side of the building to prevent escape attempts. Border guards were always on the street and the residents had to apply for a pass for their visitors at the police station before they could enter. So no spontaneous visits to friends? When one of these flats became empty, mostly because of a death, they were never rented out again despite there being a serious housing shortage. At some point all the houses on the western side of the street were empty. The west-facing windows in all buildings near the Wall were usually bricked up over time.

The question often arose in discussions among those who enjoyed to philosophise as to who was "imprisoned" by the Wall because it could be said that West Berlin was like one big open prison. You could of course move around freely within the confines of the Wall just getting on with your daily life. It was when you wanted to go further afield that you were reminded of the political situation. That was most noticeable in summer if you wanted to head out of the city for the day.

Many day-trippers headed to somewhere like Lake Wannsee or to one of the many lovely parks in West Berlin for a day out. Going beyond the border wasn't worth it for a day because of the time it took to get to the West. For longer breaks you could fly out of Tegel airport, an easy way to get off the "island." It was when leaving by road or rail that the often time consuming and annoying checks and controls imposed on you would cause you to reflect on your standing and freedom of movement.

First visit to East Berlin

In contrast to those living in the "high security prison" which was the East, you did however have the choice of leaving when you wanted.

There was a compulsory exchange amount of 25 DM per day in place when crossing to the East which allowed the East Germans to get their hands on Deutschmarks, (hard currency). The problem was that there was little you could spend the East Marks on and it was illegal to take any East Marks back to the West. Some people got round this by going out for a meal which cost next to nothing but was of questionable quality and wasn't an option for a vegetarian. If you spoke and read German then you could always spend the eastern currency on books.

Through time I became aware that there was an unofficial exchange rate where you could get something like 4 East Marks or more for 1 DM. It was of course illegal but that probably made it more enticing for most. For West Berliners (as opposed to foreigners living there) a separate system was in place if they wanted to visit East Berlin. They couldn't be spontaneous about it as they had to apply for a visa in advance.

From Palace to police

The weather wasn't too good that day for walking around so we decided to go into the Palace of the Republic a very impressive new building on Unter den Linden. The outside of the Palace was like coppered glass and literally dazzling (it was knocked down after reunification – see note below).

We had certainly picked the right time for a visit as a town called Karl Marx Stadt (since renamed Chemnitz) was putting on a three day festival. There was a full orchestra playing and a variety of dancers dazzled in their beautiful costumes. The orchestra played a broad variety of music styles, everything from the theme from 'Saturday Night Fever' to Strauss waltzes. It was a really fantastic display. Most of the activity took place on the ground floor which was overlooked by galleries so that we had a great view of the entire spectacle from our position on the upper level. There were amazing lamps suspended from the high ceiling on cords of different lengths creating clusters of light at varying heights. Huge paintings hung from the walls.

In the evening there were two or three discos on but we discovered that we hadn't enough money for the entrance fee. When it became obvious to the organisers that we were foreigners, they let us in free. The main hall was like something out of a dream the dinner tables being beautifully decorated with fine tablecloths and posies of flowers adorned each one. There were two bands and various singers in the main hall and two separate discos in other rooms. It was all so beautiful that it seemed unreal. We were enjoying ourselves so much that we felt like Cinderella when we had to leave at 11.30pm in order to be back at Checkpoint Charlie by midnight. We only had a day pass.

From Palace to police

When we left that fairytale environment to re-enter the real world we had a good idea of how Cinderella must have felt as the contrast was so stark. The streets were completely dark and empty and it looked as though they rolled up the pavements at 6pm anyway. Not a single car could be seen or even heard in the distance. It was eerily quiet. At that time you had to wait around 8-10 years to buy a car, not because you needed that time to save the money but that was how long you had to wait for one to become available. They just didn't produce enough to meet demand.

We were approaching the wide crossroads at Leipziger Strasse near Checkpoint Charlie on our way back to the border crossing and as there wasn't a soul about we walked across the road without waiting for the wee green man in the traffic lights to show up. Big mistake. Out of thin air, a member of the East German Peoples' Police *Volkspolizist* appeared complete with gun (they all carried them). Peoples' police is certainly a misnomer as like any police force, they are not there for the people.

At that time Steve spoke better German than I and he translated saying that we were being fined for jaywalking, crossing the road whilst the wee green man was red. (illegal in both East and West). In West Berlin you could spot the foreigners as they just looked both ways and crossed an empty street at 3am whilst Germans were obediently standing at a traffic light waiting for the wee red man to put on his green suit. I guess we are not as orderly or obedient as the Germans because if we had such laws in the UK then the police would have a full time job fining every second person as most people cross a street anywhere after checking that it is safe to do so.

I was indignant and said to Steve that I wasn't going to pay any fines for something so stupid but Steve had a bit more knowledge of the system than I and pointed out that if we didn't pay we might have difficulty getting out again. The thought of being detained in the East didn't appeal to me at all so we reluctantly coughed up.

It wasn't the amount we were fined, five Deutschmarks (West Marks) each (I still have the receipt) but the principle of it. We had just spent such a magical day in East Berlin and this was how the day had ended. We later learned that this was a tourist trap, a way for the East Germans to easily earn hard currency. They knew that anyone they stopped was easy prey as you had no choice but to pay the fine. Nobody would have wanted to be arrested by them and ending up in an East German prison was a horror scenario, something to be avoided at all costs.

So apart from our magical time in the Palace of the Republic which was like stepping into another world, my abiding impression of the East was that everything was grey, even the people. There was little colour anywhere apart from the colours offered by nature and they were in short supply at that time of year. They didn't have the lights and bright signs that you saw in the West nor did the buildings have colourful facades.

Palace of the Republic

In 1990 the Palace of the Republic was closed after the discovery of asbestos. The concentration of asbestos fibres was found to be way above the acceptable safe level. Work to remove the asbestos began in 1998 and took several years to complete. However in 2003 the German Parliament decided it would have to be demolished, despite interest groups opposing such a decision. The death sentence had been passed and the fate of the Palace of the Republic was sealed. At around the same time the Foreign Ministry of the GDR which stood opposite was also torn down.

You wonder why on earth it was decided to demolish the Palace of the Republic *after* a considerable amount of money must surely have been spent on removing the asbestos? I suspect that the iconic building was always a source of annoyance for the West being seen as symbolic of the GDR. It had been the seat of the GDR Parliament and all the SED (communist) party conferences took place there. But it had also been a popular destination for GDR citizens to go dancing, eat out or attend cultural events.

Schönebergerstrasse

When Steve's girlfriend Linda moved to Berlin, I moved out and stayed temporarily with a few other people before moving into a flatshare with an English guy called Dave at number 18 Schönebergerstrasse. The flat was on the fourth floor in the back house and had a bathroom which was built onto part of the kitchen whilst the resident on the other side of the stairs had an outside toilet on the landing. Obviously both flats had originally shared the outside toilet.

Schönebergerstrasse is beside Gleisdreieck underground station in Kreuzberg. There were two levels to this station, and both tracks ran above ground but the lower level had a line to nowhere being a line which had previously gone to East Berlin. In common with many such lines, it was no longer used after the Wall went up. The upper line used to be line 1 which went from Ruhleben to Schleschisches Tor. The track was high above the ground so that travelling on that line gave you a great view over the rooftops. I raced up the more than a hundred steps to this line many times as the approaching train could be heard or seen as it neared the station.

There were very few flats in the area so mostly, but especially at night, your footsteps would be the only ones echoing along the dark, deserted platform as you made your way from the train to the street or vice versa. The station and whole surrounding area was also very poorly lit and could have been used as a film set from the 50s just as it was, as it didn't look as though much of it had changed since that era.

Schönebergerstrasse

Berlin has always exuded a sense of mystery, intrigue and decadence. In the dark of winter this aura of mysteriousness seemed heightened as everything appeared as though viewed through a subtle mist. It wasn't obviously real mist but people and things seemed to have this air of being not quite tangible, as though just behind a thin veil. It had something to do with the haze around the streetlamps and the soft light they bestowed on everything. It was certainly very atmospheric. It is still like that today whereas sadly in most parts of Scotland, light pollution has stolen the darkness.

Learning German

The system for teaching foreign languages isn't particularly good, at least not in the UK so although I had learnt German for a couple of years in school I could only speak a few words of German upon my arrival in Berlin. I got busy with a cassette and book and studied every single day, but mixing with Germans in those days was a big obstacle to learning German because they all wanted to practise their English. I don't know if you have ever tried to learn a language but when foreigners want to practise their command of your language and they can speak it better than you can theirs then there is a tendency to give up. For that reason I didn't really become proficient in German until a couple of years later.

In 1981 I went to a language school in the morning for a couple of months to learn the grammar (German grammar is not easy for a lot of Germans let alone native English speakers) and then I got a job working in a pub at night. There's nothing like talking to lots of different people to help you learn a language. We all use colloquial vocabulary and phrases so working in

Schönebergerstrasse

places like clubs and pubs is a great way to learn. My shift in the pub finished at 3am, opening hours unheard of in Scotland at that time. After clearing up, I had a 20 minute walk home. Even though there were night trains and buses, Schöneberger-strasse was a place which was awkward to get to by bus so it was sometimes quicker to walk or cycle home. Although the underground station Gleisdreieck was a couple of minutes walk from my flat, the trains weren't very frequent at that time in the morning so if you had just missed one then it was quicker to walk than wait for the next one. I never at any time had any fear of walking through Berlin at that early hour.

I didn't realise then that my ability to speak German would later lead to a job in East Berlin at the British Embassy. Nor could I have imagined that in the not too distant future crossing Checkpoint Charlie or other border crossings between East and West Berlin on a daily basis would become a normal daily occurrence for me.

.

British Embassy

In December 1982 I started work in the British Embassy in East Berlin which at that time was situated on *Unter den Linden* (under the Lindens). If you have never been to Berlin, *Unter den Linden* is the lovely wide boulevard which begins at Brandenburg Gate and ends at the Berlin Cathedral. There is a central walkway along part of the boulevard and it could be considered as East Berlin's equivalent of the Champs Elysees in Paris.

Before the city was divided, *Unter den Linden* was probably the most important street in Berlin with a lively nightlife and the place to be seen by those who placed importance on such things. This historical street which still has some beautiful old buildings was, and fortunately still is, bordered in places by Linden trees from which it takes its name. In summer, when the Linden trees are in full bloom there is a heavenly scent in the whole street. I used to love coming out of the Embassy to be elevated to a different level by that beautiful perfume which seemed to envelop me like a cocoon as though to say, "Breathe in the beauty and leave the crap of the day behind you."

The passable German I spoke at that time was instrumental in my getting the job in the Embassy as the British are not known for their foreign language skills. Learning even a few phrases in another language opens up the culture in a way that expecting others to speak English doesn't. Now of course so many people do speak English because of the influence of the computing world and the internet.

I was one of the so-called 'locally engaged' in the Embassy. We weren't diplomats or civil servants and lived in West Berlin although our official address as far as the East Germans were concerned was at the Embassy. The East German authorities knew of course that we didn't live at the Embassy but this was one of the little games governments played. We had two passports, our official one and one for Embassy use which was renewed yearly.

There were about seven of us locally engaged. We were secretaries, drivers, clerks etc. We had what I called pseudo diplomatic number plates for our cars (the plates were red and started with CY as opposed to CD for diplomats) and we couldn't be stopped or searched by the East Germans. We could of course be stopped and searched by the British, French and Americans as they "controlled" West Berlin. We drove across the border every day, mostly at Checkpoint Charlie although there were other border crossings such as Heinrich Heine Strasse or Invalidenstrasse which we could have used. It depended really on which part of West Berlin you lived in and which crossing was nearest your home but most, as far as I know, crossed at Checkpoint Charlie. We went through a special channel at the border and didn't have to queue up with other cars going across.

Crossing from East to West Berlin was like time travelling. It felt like leaving the 60s and entering the 80s. The East was so grey and colourless but as soon as you got to the West there were bursts of colour everywhere, brightly painted shops signs, neon lights, colourful clothes and the colours of nature. It seemed to me as though even the very air changed at the border. You left the east air which stank of Trabis and entered the west air which didn't. Logically of course, the air merged but I was always fascinated by the impression that there was some kind of invisible curtain which not only separated people but the very air they breathed.

It was a strange situation being a border crosser spending my working days in the East and the rest of my life in the West of Berlin. When walking about the East you really stuck out as it was obvious from your clothing your hairstyle and demeanour that you weren't "one of them." I didn't get the feeling that it would have been a good idea to approach people even if it were simply to seek directions. A simple gesture such as smiling at people as you caught their eye in passing was made difficult anyway as most tended to avoid eye contact in that way.

I vividly remember my first few months at the Embassy. At that time I didn't own a car and travelled to work by underground exiting at Friedrichstrasse Station. This was one of the border controls where anyone with a visa or diplomatic pass could cross. I used to feel really sorry for the citizens of East Berlin whom I saw near the departure hall at Friedrichstrasse station. They were saying goodbye to friends or family who had been visiting from the West but they of course couldn't leave the East. It was heart wrenching to witness the emotional distress of both parties and it upset me quite a lot. I often arrived at the Embassy with tears in my eyes. There is now a museum there which is called *Tränenpalast* – Palace of tears, I can understand the tears bit but can't imagine why anyone would want to call it a Palace.

Initially I was engaged as secretary to both the Commercial Attaché and the Cultural Attaché. Normally the Cultural Attaché would work out of the British Council offices but there were no such offices in East Berlin. If the British Council had been allowed to open a Cultural centre in East Berlin then the East Germans would have demanded a cultural centre somewhere in the UK. There was no way the British Government was prepared to do that so for that reason, the Cultural Attaché was based in the British Embassy. After a few months I worked exclusively for the Cultural Attaché as his workload had increased, (He was out and about a lot and a fluent Russian speaker). I found the cultural side much more interesting than commerce so I was happy about that

My security clearance in the Embassy permitted me to handle documents or information up to a *restricted* level. If there was anything which needed typed with that classification I wasn't allowed to type it in my office, I had to go to a wee windowless room upstairs (where none of the East German staff were allowed to enter) to use an old manual typewriter. It was like sitting in a cupboard.

Trained typists use all five digits. With old manual typewriters you had to use a fair amount of pressure on every key but as the strength in each of our fingers varies it makes the striking of each key irregular. We also had to use carbon paper to make copies so if you made a mistake then white correcting fluid was applied to the top copy but not the carbon copy. The electric typewriters in use at the time required less pressure to depress the keys giving a more even striking of them all. We were told that this resulted in anything typed on an electric typewriter being easier to decipher by the East Germans with the eavesdropping equipment they had available at that time. At least that is what we were told.

British Embassy

I presume there must have been some kind of agreement with the East Germans which stipulated that every foreign Embassy or Representation had to employ some East German staff. I am sure they were expected to gather as much information on us as they could. Some were definitely more zealous about it than others.

Working in an Embassy or Consulate, particularly one from a Western Country, had several advantages for the East German Employees: They had the opportunity to use and improve their foreign language speaking skills, as the lack of contact with native speakers meant that their knowledge of foreign languages was theoretical: They had access to information, magazines and newspapers from the West which would otherwise have been denied them and in some Embassies they received a small amount of pocket money in Deutschmarks with which they could occasionally buy western goods from the *Intershop*. (The Intershop stocked western goods which couldn't be found in any shops in the East eg electrical goods, western food and clothing and payment could only be made in Deutschmarks). Working in Embassies or Diplomatic Missions wasn't however the most lucrative of jobs. In contrast Workers in some of the big factories which were extremely important from an economic viewpoint had several advantages such as getting a flat or car or valuable consumer goods.

Some East German citizens were paid by the Stasi to spy on friends, family and colleagues and they could earn the equivalent of a month's salary for doing so. Others were forced into spying. I found that, of the few East Germans I got to know, most tended to be "two-faced." It was the only way to cope with the system really. The ones who weren't hard line party members had to project an image externally which didn't sit with who they really were but what choice did they have under such a regime? They had to play the system in the same way as the system played them. Those who couldn't cope with living under such a totalitarian government usually ended up in prison if they went against it or tried to escape the country. If the escape attempt was unsuccessful then they usually ended up dead.

One important difference between the citizens of East and West I found was that the citizens of the East were painfully aware that they didn't live in a democracy and tailored their behaviour to suit, if they wanted to exist within the system. The citizens in the West however thought they lived in a democracy, a 'free' country, as most do today and were therefore much easier to control and fool. So which ones do you think were/are the wisest?

None are so hopelessly enslaved as those who falsely believe they are free. -Goethe

Spies in our midst

There were two East Germans employed at the Embassy. They dealt with correspondence in German and advised on protocol but were without doubt also expected to gather as much information as possible on everyone which they would of course pass on to the Stasi. One of the two women who worked there was almost certainly married to a member of the Party because he often travelled abroad with his job and no ordinary East citizen would have had that freedom. The other woman who was there when I started was Claudia. I really liked Claudia she had a very gentle nature. Unfortunately she was "removed" not long after I started as she obviously wasn't passing on sufficient information to her minders. I remember the day she told me about it, she was really upset.

Interestingly Claudia and I met again eight years later whilst I was managing the East Side Gallery. At that time she was working for a Japanese TV company and had come to interview me at the Gallery.

Note: in 2018 I was delighted to track Claudia down and below she tells the story of her removal from the Embassy in her own words.

Relationships

I could never understand the behaviour which I observed amongst most of the diplomats. The relationships amongst Embassy staff, not just those in the British Embassy, bordered on the incestuous as they primarily socialised with each other. Few of them appeared to have any interest in meeting socially with Germans unless they were also diplomats. When I visit or live in a foreign country then there is no way I want to spend all my time with other Brits. I want to mix with the natives and learn about their culture. Obviously in East Germany socialising with the natives wasn't encouraged but the diplomats in East Berlin could easily have struck up friendships with Germans in the west part of Berlin. In my experience however that rarely happened.

There was also a lot of snobbishness within the British Embassy. The diplomats often looked down on other members of staff, their colleagues. Within the Embassy you were reminded of the ridiculous British class system as it was very much on display there. I am sure this is a great sense of amusement for most other nations who find it incredulous that we even have a first and second class delivery in our postal service.

Whilst employed by the Embassy I could travel about East Berlin fairly easily although it was preferred if you didn't do this on your own. I could apply in advance for visas for friends or family to visit the East but didn't do this often. So travelling in the East with friends from the West wasn't really something you could do spontaneously.

<u>Leipzig</u>

I had been to Leipzig in East Germany on several occasions as the British Embassy had a stand at the Leipzig trade fair which took place twice a year and my East German colleagues and I had to work there. We drove there in Embassy vehicles and if Erich Honecker was going to be at the Fair we had to plan our departure time carefully. When Honecker was driving in his cavalcade then all other cars were made to stop at the side of the road until he passed. This meant either leaving long before or shortly after Honecker and his entourage to avoid having an enforced rest at the side of the road.

It took a brave East German to come onto the British stand at Leipzig because after they left they would be followed and interrogated by the Stasi therefore most were too afraid to do so. The same thing happened if they had the courage to come into the Embassy. We probably only had one or two East

British Embassy

German teachers of English brave enough to come onto the stand desperately seeking any kind of printed material in English. Their command of our language was pretty bad but this wasn't surprising as the poor souls had no access to any kind of English language magazines or newspapers and no opportunity to converse with a native English speaker in their private lives. The easiest and quickest way to learn a foreign language is to immerse yourself in the language by spending time in the country where it is spoken. A slower method of learning is talking to a native of that country on a regular basis or reading printed material; these options were denied GDR citizens.

When the Stasi came onto the stand it took me all my time not to laugh at them as you could spot them a mile away. They always seemed to be dressed from head to toe in brown - brown trousers, brown shoes and jackets. However, I learned later that this was intentional as the Stasi were very clever and ruthless and the ones in brown were probably a decoy. Erich Honecker once came onto the British stand whilst I was there and before his arrival one of his minions came to test whatever he would be offered to drink to make sure it wasn't poisoned. It reminded me of aeons ago when the King would have someone taste everything he ate and drank to make sure it wasn't poisoned. I just couldn't take this seriously and the more seriously they took it, the more I wanted to laugh.

As a vegetarian my food supply when going to Leipzig for a few days took up more space than the case with my clothes. The food in East Germany was pretty dire in general and a vegetarian would have starved to death. Any fresh vegetables on sale were seasonal and they were usually anything but fresh. East German citizens joked that the reason they were so fond of sweet things and sugar was because the rest of the food was so awful. Fortunately my two East German colleagues and I were put up in a flat whilst in Leipzig so we had basic cooking facilities.

GDR citizens didn't go hungry as staple foods were very cheap but there was little variety, choice was a luxury. This also meant that food and other commodities weren't wasted. After the "wave" of recognition of the GDR as an official country in the 70s a delicatessen was opened in Berlin where western foods could be bought with East Marks but the prices were extortionate. You could pay in the region of 14.00 East Marks for a tin of pineapples, prices which were totally out of reach of the average worker. At the beginning of the 80s such shops were opened in other cities such as Leipzig and Dresden; places which attracted many tourists. Later it was possible to buy clothing from the West in the *Exquisit* shops where payment was in East Marks but horrendously expensive.

On one of those trips to the Leipzig Fair I recall glancing into the train station as I passed one of its entrances and seeing a man in uniform standing there. There was no one else around and the usual complete absence of any colour. It was almost as though I had been transported back in time to the last war as he could quite easily have walked out of a photo of that era. I can still see that image quite clearly.

I revisited Leipzig in 2018 and what a lovely city it is. The huge train station is a magnificent building and has been completely transformed since my visit in the 80s. In the late 80s many of the old blocks of flats there still bore the wounds of bullet holes from the Second World War and in common with many other places in East Germany were in a sad state of disrepair. There was simply no will to repair them and new housing was invested in instead.

You may have gathered that working for the British Government wasn't my dream job. I enjoyed it for a couple of years as the diplomatic staff stayed for about two years before they moved on so there were always changes and that suited me.

It turned out that the British Embassy was far removed from being a fair employer. As locally engaged staff we were led to believe that we were better off than the staff in the British Consulate in West Berlin because we didn't pay tax. We were told that we were "compensated" for having to cross the border every day. It turned out that this wasn't the case at all.

It may sound a wonderful idea not to pay tax but for us it certainly wasn't as we had to pay for private health insurance and no contributions were paid to our Retirement Pensions whilst employed by the Embassy. Paying income tax does have certain advantages. When I brought this up with the Ambassador he more or less said if you don't like it then leave. I then made enquiries about joining the West German system and paying contributions to them but was told this wasn't possible. I also wrote to a Union in the UK but that turned out to be a complete waste of time. We were really in no man's land and nobody cared about us.

British Embassy

Competent is not the first word which springs to mind when recalling some of the Diplomatic staff, whether they were employed at the Embassy or merely visiting. It is interesting how governmental staff at all levels rarely seem to have been chosen for their abilities. Perhaps the main selection criterion is willingness to obey. It is very difficult to respect that. After four years I decided to leave. I had become fed up with the feeling of always being watched and I remember we once got a letter recommending we check under our vehicles for bombs. I suspect that made up my mind to go sooner rather than later.

My last year in the Embassy was 1986. There were articles in the papers about East Germans seeking asylum in the American Embassy which was located round the corner from the British one but not a word about them also being in the British Embassy. I remember going to work one morning and a guy came out of the internal security door of the Embassy carrying his toothbrush and towel and went into a small interview room just inside the front entrance door. So, the British Embassy also had East Germans wanting to leave. I have no idea what happened to them.

Claudia Linde

My employment at the British Embassy, East Berlin from autumn 1980 to December 1983

After completing my studies at the Karl-Marx University in Leipzig I was assigned to the Service Provider for Foreign Representations (*Dienstleistungsamt für Ausländische Vertretungen*) in East Berlin in September 1976. In the GDR it was common practice for graduates to commit themselves to go wherever they were most urgently needed, from an economic viewpoint and to stay there for at least three years. That applied to the locality as well as to the business. I was happy to be going to Berlin as it was exactly what I wanted. I didn't want to wither away in some *Intertext* office (the GDR Government's language translation service) because after my English language studies my strong point was in the oral use of the language.

The Service Provider for Foreign Representations was a branch of the GDR Foreign Ministry. At the end of 1972 the basic treaty between the Federal Republic of Germany (West Germany) and the GDR was ratified. It regulated the relations of both German states and it was agreed to establish a permanent representation of the Federal Republic of Germany in the GDR. Both German states became members of the UN in March 1973.

This was accompanied by a wave of international recognition of the GDR. Within a short time, the GDR not only had to provide suitable buildings for the establishment of embassies and residences, but also had to recruit qualified (GDR) personnel to work in the embassies and trade missions. That was the task of the Service Provider. Staff, such as housekeepers, cooks and butlers were sought for the ambassadors' residences and in the embassies drivers, caretakers and office workers with appropriate language skills were employed. I don't know whether the embassies were actually obliged to hire GDR personnel but I think it is quite possible.

I had worked as a secretary/interpreter in various embassies and commercial offices since 1976 (staying an average of 2 years). After that I wanted to go where I chose and that was relatively quickly achieved through my employment with the Service Provider. Bit by bit I had extended my English vocabulary which now went beyond the terms and phrases learnt for translating at SED Party conferences or other political events and developments. The focus of my language studies was in being able to explain the political and economic development and goals of the GDR and not in learning the everyday English spoken by people in normal life.

In the spring of 1980 I finally got a small flat in the Prenzlauer Berg area, which was arranged by the Service Provider. Up to that point I had lived in a type of hostel which was owned by the Service Provider and many of their employees were housed there. Those who were working for the Service Provider got flats easier and were so to speak privileged. Living space was scarce in the GDR and only those who had a family or perhaps like me worked in a foreign agency were given preferential housing. Normally you had to apply for an apartment at the district Council office (for Berlin) and sometimes it took more than 10 years as a single person before you were allocated something. This preferential treatment certainly had something to do with the Service Provider's reputation within the foreign representations as they were eager to be seen as looking after their employees. It was obvious that people were going to talk about aspects of their private life whilst at work so on that subject we could honestly say that the Service Provider took care of its employees.

Often flats were placed in new buildings, which were built especially for embassy employees. New Embassies and Residences were built, particularly in the Pankow district. I was really happy to finally escape from the hostel as you always felt you were under surveillance there. My new flat was situated in the back house and near Prenzlauer Allee S-Bahn station. The flat consisted of 1.5 rooms which meant one big room, my living room and a small room of about 8 sqm which served as a bedroom and although it had oven (coal) heating there was at least an inside toilet with a small sink.

Up until May/June 1980 I had worked for an Indian commercial company. In the spring of 1980 the Commercial Representative who had been there for many years was replaced. Unfortunately the working atmosphere went downhill after his replacement arrived as we just didn't get on. For this reason I asked the Service Provider for a transfer. My wish was quickly granted as it transpired that the Representative in question had already been in contact with the Service Provider with the request that a colleague and I be replaced.

I had booked a long trip for that July through the GDR Youth Travel Agency and I was therefore glad to leave everything behind me for three weeks. That journey took me to North Korea and it was the most interesting trip I ever had in my youth. Our guide was a member of the Free German Youth Council (*Freie Deutsche Jugend*=FDJ) and most certainly one or the other traveller was working for the state security but I didn't care. As a citizen of the GDR you could only travel abroad by booking a trip with the state travel agency and you could only go to those socialist countries which were in alliance with the GDR like Poland, Soviet Union (now Russia), Czech Republic, Romania, Bulgaria and Hungary.

Claudia Linde

On my return from holiday I was initially employed in the administration of the Service Provider and was sent out to various Embassies on short term assignments. I could hardly believe my luck when in the autumn of 1980 the Service Provider hired me out to the British Embassy in East Berlin. The fact that my "group instructor" (Kaderinstrukteur) was already at that point preparing me for possible espionage ("keep your eyes and ears open") had simply gone over my head.

In the GDR the British Embassy was situated at 32-34 Unter den Linden. In the beginning I worked in an office which was shared with two other GDR secretaries and an English colleague and we carried out general administrative duties. These duties included writing letters, completing invitation lists and arranging appointments for the Ambassador with the various Ministries etc. A few weeks after arriving there I joined the Commercial section. In addition to three GDR secretaries there was also a GDR driver employed by the Embassy. The rest of the administrative personnel were all British. In the Embassy's Commercial section I was therefore the only German. My tasks were to translate short texts from German into English, type letters and to arrange appointments with the relevant partners in the GDR Ministries and to follow articles in the GDR press about the economy.

The British Embassy, through the British Chamber of Commerce, took a large stand at the Leipzig Trade Fair which took place twice yearly. This meant for me that I had to work at every Leipzig Trade Fair on behalf of the Embassy. (This was anything but a chore for me as I had had to work at the Leipzig Trade Fair during my studies in order to put my language skills into practice.) We even received a new "uniform" every time which consisted of a skirt and blouse which was worn by all the female personnel on the stand and they were bought in the West. For me it was always like a precious present and I wore the blouses and skirts for a very long time after the relevant Fair. It was something special you couldn't find in the GDR's shopping centres. Even today, more than thirty years later I still have one or two blouses from that time.

The first time I worked on stand GB in 1981, everything went like clockwork. I met two other GDR colleagues who had worked on a stand at the Fair for a few years longer than I and we always had a really interesting time together. I was allowed to accompany business people from Britain to their appointments with GDR foreign trade companies and to interpret for them. The Stand was more or less closed off and had only a very small reception area for the "public" and now and again a GDR visitor to the Fair would find their way there in the hope of perhaps getting a few travel brochures.

In the spring of 1982 or to be more exact at the beginning of March, shortly before the Spring Trade Fair my doorbell rang one evening. At that time I had one close friend but no serious boyfriend so I lived a very quiet life. At first I was completely shocked because I had been reading the *Woman's Own*, *Spiegel* and *Stern* magazines which I was allowed to borrow from the Embassy even though being in possession of or even reading western magazines was strictly forbidden for citizens of East Germany. I opened the door to find two men standing there who showed me their Identity cards and introduced themselves as members of the Ministry for State Security (Stasi). I let them in and hastily hid my "west" magazines. After some general small talk they got to the real reason for the visit. They knew that I went to the Leipzig Trade Fair every year with the British Embassy to work on their stand. They informed me that for the Spring Fair this year it was planned that a visit be made to the British Stand by a delegation from the Government which was to be headed by the Secretary General, Erich Honecker. For this reason they asked me to take particular care and attention so that the visit would go smoothly and that the life and limb of the Secretary General was not endangered. The words of my "group instructor" (Kaderinstrukteur) as he was preparing me for my assignment in the British Embassy came back to me then. My stomach tensed up immediately as these two Stasi Majors relayed their demand but I had no counter argument with which to escape this appeal to protect Erich Honecker.

Somehow or other I had been expecting the Stasi to make contact with me for some time but now that it was real and had happened so suddenly I was speechless. I told them that since I was a child special occasions whether pleasant or otherwise always upset my stomach. The effect went from not being able to eat to feeling sick all day. That was my argument for leaving it at a one-off support. However I didn't want to forego the opportunity to ask what was in it for me (new flat). They remained reserved and asked initially that I fulfil this one assignment. We arranged to meet again in Leipzig during the Trade Fair. The meeting was to take place in the evening near the *Grassi Museum*. Those days at the Fair were really stressful for me. I felt really unwell but there was no-one I could confide in.

Finally the day of the Government delegation's visit to our stand arrived. Two Security/Stasi members came onto the stand more than two hours before Erich Honecker and his delegates were due. They checked out the entire stand to ensure there were no corners where anything could be hidden. It had been agreed that Erich Honecker would be offered a glass of sekt during his conversation with the Ambassador to toast the good relationship between the GDR and Britain. The two Stasi men became "tasters" when they drank some sekt and the glasses had to be filled in their presence after which they never let the bottle out of their sight for a second until the arrival of Erich Honecker and the Ambassador. We, the personnel, had to remain in the background.

On the evening of my agreed meeting with the Stasi the weather was dreadful, it was pouring rain and it was dark. I was shaking from head to toe as I walked along the row of parked cars at the *Grassi Museum* when suddenly headlights flashed briefly and I knew then that it must be them in what I recognised as a Lada. When I got into the car I found myself sitting with three men only one of whom I recognised from our first meeting. I was thanked for the part I played in making the visit to the British Stand so successful. It was taken for granted that my further assistance within the Embassy/Commercial department could be counted on. I was absolutely sure at that point that I didn't want to do any more. I made it very clear that psychologically I was being forced into a corner and that the resulting mental stress would destroy me physically. I told them that I wasn't able to eat properly for days before the meeting and that I would collapse if I had to carry out any further assignments. Initially they accepted that, which greatly surprised me. However I was advised to think it all over as it was after all about the safety of the GDR and the British Embassy. A further meeting in my home sometime in April 1982 was agreed. That meeting was very relaxed although the two Stasi officers still tried to win me over for further collaboration. Their argument was that, "The Ministry, by way of agreements and contracts agreed under international Law, was also responsible for the protection and safety of privileged persons and their property whilst in the GDR" (quote from my Stasi file). Once again I made it clear that I didn't want any further contact because psychologically I wouldn't be able to cope with it. No further meeting was arranged. Later I learned from my Stasi file that the Ministry for State Security had already logged me as a candidate for unofficial collaboration with the code name "Simone."

I really enjoyed my job at the British Embassy as it became more and more interesting and I finally had the opportunity to speak proper English. I couldn't attend the Leipzig Trade Fair in the autumn of 1982 as I was unwell but I attended both Fairs in the spring and autumn of 1983. Although I was sharing a privately rented flat there with Christine, my colleague from the Embassy and the author of this book, I was never approached by the Stasi again.*

After the autumn 1983 Fair the atmosphere in the Commercial department changed suddenly. I was called into the office of my boss at that time, the First Commercial secretary. He was really upset and confided in me that the Service Provider had contacted the Embassy with the ultimatum that I was to be removed from the Embassy immediately. He asked if I knew of

Claudia Linde

any possible reason and I then told him the whole story of what I had experienced through contact with the Stasi. He said that he had suspected as much and would inform the Ambassador accordingly. He also fully understood that caution would have to be taken with my potential successor.

The Ambassador pleaded with the GDR Foreign Ministry for me to remain in the British Embassy stating that I was indispensable from the perspective of the further development of commercial relations between the GDR and Britain and couldn't just be removed from the Commercial Department from one day to the next. The Service Provider justified the recall by citing a "rotation system." The Ambassador was actually successful in my being allowed to carry on working in the Embassy until the end of 1983 and even held a wonderful farewell meal for me in his residence to which many British diplomats but no GDR personnel were invited. I found it very difficult to take my leave of the Embassy staff and I believe many of them felt the same. The Service Provider had very quickly found a successor for me and I had already been informed by them that my next placement would be in the Japanese Embassy and would begin in January 1984. This position turned out to be really lucky, especially after the "Wende"........

* in my Stasi file there was a sort of final evaluation dated July 1983. I was appraised as "not suitable for conspiratorial activities."

Claudia Linde

Berlin housing

Christine's Story

Prior to my arrival in Berlin, I had lived most of my life in houses so the housing landscape in Berlin was completely different to anything I had known. I had lived in flats in Glasgow and East Kilbride for a short while but there tends to be a mix of houses and flats in many of the districts there. In Berlin, houses tended to be owned by the rich and/or powerful and were on the outskirts, places like Grünewald and Wannsee whereas blocks of flats were more common elsewhere. The homes were far bigger than those in Scotland. Any Germans I have spoken to who have visited Scotland are amazed at how small our homes are in comparison to those in Germany. The Germans have a far more intelligent system for charging rents or setting a purchase price for property because the cost is determined by the price per square metre, unlike the nonsensical British system whereby it is the number of bedrooms a property has, irrespective of their size, which determines the rent or purchase price!

I discovered that in common with most places in Europe people tended to rent rather than buy their homes. The system enabled them to rent a property for as long as they wanted. It was completely different to the UK where people were often forced into debt by taking out mortgages to buy homes because the monthly repayment was less than the expensive, predominantly private rents and at times little or no deposit was necessary. Many Council houses in the UK were being sold off cheaply to sitting tenants so their number was constantly shrinking making it easier for unscrupulous private landlords to charge extortionate rents.

Berlin housing

Unfortunately the Berlin rental situation is changing for the worse and more properties are being purchased often by foreign buyers for purely speculative purposes. This is now drastically increasing rents to an unaffordable level for anyone on an average salary. The Berliners have a culture of sharing properties with other people who are not necessarily friends. The large rooms in old properties are well suited to such a lifestyle. Even allowing for this sharing culture, finding an affordable room or entire flat to rent in Berlin has now become extremely difficult. This is despite the rent ceiling in place which regulates how much rent per square metre may be charged. It is a case of supply and demand which is of course exploited by many landlords. When a tenant moves out whoever moves in is given a new contract with a usually greatly increased rent.

Many of the old apartment blocks were four storeys high and without lifts. There were also terms like front and back house, back house right or left and even second back house that I had to learn. It wasn't sufficient to have someone's house number if you wanted to visit; you needed precise information as to where in the house they lived. Also, if someone were a subtenant then it was possible their name was not even on the doorbell so you also needed the name of the tenant so you could ring the correct bell. (For anyone brought up with mobile phones this concept is probably difficult to grasp as you would simply phone when you got there).

Berlin housing

Front house meant facing the street and there would often be one or more rear courtyards so that when you entered the back court (often via a separate side door, some large enough to drive through) you would have flats on the right and left, like wings. Straight ahead there might then be a wall or there might be another courtyard beyond that with more flats on the right and left. The cellars were usually accessed from the courtyard.

The houses at the front originally extended to part of those back wings maybe that is where the servants had lived because you didn't get much daylight there the only windows being those overlooking the courtyard. As well as cutting down the amount of light and sunlight you got, it also meant you didn't have windows at both sides of the flat to open to allow a very necessary through draught in the heat of Berlin's summers, when the temperature can reach +38°C. The front of the block at street level could be quite ornate, and the flats usually had balconies, unlike those in the back court. The windows facing the front street were also double, not double glazing but two separate sets of windows with a gap of about 3 inches (8cm) between them. The back wings were completely plain and functional and the windows were single. The rooms in old front houses were often decorated with lovely stucco and ornate cornices on the ceilings, something I never saw in a flat situated at the back of a building.

The way old flats had been divided up often created strange shaped rooms. In 1990 I was living in a flat in Yorckstrasse in the Kreuzberg district. The flat had two rooms at the front facing onto Yorckstrasse and then two rooms at the back. One, the kitchen, faced onto the back courtyard and the other extended into part of a back wing. I assume at one point it stretched the length of the back wing. There was a triangular shaped room at this point with a corner window. This was where the bath was; the triangular space left enough room to get in and out of the bath and that was it. The toilet in that flat was at the end of a wide hall and was literally a raised throne in what was once a cupboard.

At that time, most of the old flats I lived in or visited were heated by coal which you had to carry up the stairs as the storage for the coal was in the cellar. Bear in mind these were old flats so the ceiling height was higher than in modern flats which also made the stairs more numerous.

The coal was interesting as it was either formed into a brick shape (brickets) or egg shape (eierkohl -literally egg coal). The only coal I knew from Scotland was in irregular lumps, there were no fancy shapes. The "ovens" we used to heat the apartment were also as alien to me as shaped coal. The older ovens were about 2 metres tall and tiled on the outside. (An American friend thought they were large fridges!) Some of the tiles on the oven were quite ornately decorated and in lovely colours. The brick shaped coal was used to heat these tall ovens and there was a small section on the side where you put the bricks in and another opening to remove the ash. There was also a small shelf about eye level with metal doors on the front, where you could put a pan in to warm it up. These large tiled ovens were slow burners in that they took a while to build up the heat as the bricks burned slowly but they gave off a lovely heat once you got them going. You tended to have a small top loaded oven in the kitchen for which you used the egg coal as this reached a higher heat than the bricks. In addition to heating up quicker and giving off a greater heat, you could also cook on top of it.

I am talking about the past here but these lovely old buildings still exist. Little has changed here apart from most now having central heating and perhaps locks and modern intercoms on the main entrance door to the block. Some older buildings have had lifts installed some of which go up the outside wall and are often made of glass, there being no practical way to install one within the building.

<u>Kreuzberg twice over</u>

There were two districts in West Berlin called Kreuzberg but they had different postcodes. Berliners tended to refer to them according to their postcodes so there was Kreuzberg 36 and Kreuzberg 61. Kreuzberg 36 has now joined up with the former East Berlin district of Friedrichshain for administration purposes. Many Turkish people lived in Kreuzberg 36 and opened up shops serving Turkish foods and goods. There were also many other foreigners living in Kreuzberg 36 and it was known as the arty, alternative district and was always lively and somewhat exotic. To a certain extent it still is. Sadly after the Berlin Wall opened, many of the interesting arty types who led non-conformist lives were forced out by speculators raising the rents to unaffordable levels. When the Wall surrounded West Berlin it made the city completely unattractive to property developers and similar speculators. However, once the Wall came down and the German Government moved to Berlin one of the negative changes was the level of corruption the 'new' Berlin attracted.

EAST SIDE GALLERY

The constructive phase

East Side Gallery is a 1.3km stretch of the Berlin Wall which stands in what was formerly East Berlin. The Wall *is* the Gallery. An extremely busy road with three lanes in each direction, separated by a central reservation, runs alongside it. Immediately in front of the gallery is a wide pavement. Behind the gallery, facing west, there is a strip of land on the banks of the river Spree. This strip of land was called the death strip as anyone who had managed to get over the Wall would more than likely be shot there. The death strip was pretty toxic as weedkiller was applied to it regularly to prevent the growth of vegetation. The west-facing side of the Wall was always painted white to make it easier to see would-be escapees.

The actual east/west border was on the west bank of the river, ie the whole of the river was in East Berlin territory. At some time in the life of the border there was another Wall behind the Gallery when viewed from the East. It must have been an impossible point to escape from as firstly you would have to successfully scale the "inner Wall"(as viewed from the East), ie the gallery, avoid being shot when crossing the death strip, get over the second wall and swim across the River Spree before you were safely on western territory. As soon as you left the west riverbank you were in East German territory. This bizarre situation caused the death of five children who fell into the river whilst playing on or near the riverbank. As the rescuers from the West couldn't enter the river because it was in East German territory, they had to watch the harrowing site of children drowning before their eyes. They were reliant on boats full of East German border guards coming to the rescue but by the time they arrived all that anyone could do was retrieve a lifeless body from the water.

The call of the Wall

In early January 1990 I was sharing a flat in Yorckstrasse with my friend Rita who was out of work and looking for a job. I wasn't working either at the time having spent most of 1989 attending courses and studying for my Naturopath (Heilpraktikerin) exam which I passed in September 1989. We were having one of our long, leisurely breakfasts, the table covered in lots of vegetarian delights when we started looking at the job ads in the Newspaper to see if there was anything of interest for Rita. We never did find anything to suit her but one ad immediately caught my eye, someone was looking for an assistant who could speak English for an art project on a section of the Berlin Wall situated in the East. My horoscope that day suggested I think big...........

Painting the Berlin Wall had become a kind of ritual in West Berlin, something which had to be done quickly and spontaneously to avoid being arrested. Spray painting, graffiti lent itself well to this. The only exception to this was the artist and sculptor Peter Unsicker, who over a period of three years, painted and attached sculptures and other objects to the Wall in front of his Wall-StreetGallery near Checkpoint Charlie.

There were hidden doors in the Wall and the GDR Border Guards could suddenly open them and drag you into the East so it was advisable not to work alone. Until 9th November 1989 however, it had been unimaginable to paint the side facing east, let alone a section of the Wall which stood in the east part of Berlin.

The call of the Wall

In contrast to the painting of the Wall in the West, the East Side Gallery was an organised, official project which had the permission of the custodians of the Wall and the artists were under contract to the founder of the East Side Gallery, David Monty (after Monty Python).

I was probably hooked from the moment I read the ad but it wasn't until I met David Monty or Monty as he liked to be called, that I found out about his grand plan to create the East Side Gallery or East Side Gallery **GDR** as it was originally named and the rest is history as they say. At some point the GDR was dropped from the Gallery name.

I suspect I was the only candidate who applied for the job. I don't think anyone else would have been as foolish as I was to take on a job with such complete uncertainty in every regard. Monty didn't give me a contract, there was no money and there was nothing really tangible about the arrangement but I somehow overlooked that in my enthusiasm for the project. So on 11th January 1990 I became Monty's assistant.

David Monty is what we would probably call "an interesting character." Monty called himself an Art Manager. Whatever his background, he had obtained permission from the Border Guards (who were still in charge of the Wall at that time) to allow artists to paint on the stretch of Wall in the Mühlenstrasse which became the East Side Gallery. Monty's original idea was to sell off space on a third of this section of Wall to advertisers at 1,000 DM a running metre. He suggested that some of the artists might like to earn money by painting the ads. This idea was subsequently scrapped and all the space used up for paintings.

The idea is born

On November 21st 1989, together with other artists from the GDR, Heike Stephan an East German artist, painted a piece of wall at Potsdamer Platz. It was a spontaneous action arranged by the East German Artists Association. The paintings at Potsdamer Platz were quickly painted over by the Border Guards. There was no way the authorities were going to allow the Wall to remain there. This was too near the Brandenburg Gate and no doubt plans were already made at that point to regenerate the area. I imagine the fact that this was such a lucrative piece of real estate played a large part in it.

It's a great pity they subsequently built such ugly buildings at Potsdamer Platz. It isn't as though modern architecture can't be beautiful but Potsdamer Platz resembles the extremely ugly box like constructions which were built in the 70s, with awful high rise buildings and narrow streets - nothing like the original Berlin. There is also an unpleasant energy there and it is no surprise that the underground shopping complex hasn't exactly been a resounding success. An Art Gallery formed from the Wall would have been much easier on the eye and culturally uplifting in comparison to the soulless, materialistic place this has become.

It was during this spontaneous painting action that Heike and Monty met and later that same evening Monty came up with the seemingly crazy idea to create the East Side Gallery, the largest gallery at the Wall. Heike was really enthusiastic about the idea and immediately offered her support.

The idea is born

Negotiations took place with the Border Guards and in early December 1989 Press releases gave Monty and Heike publicity for their plan for which there was neither money nor at that point official approval. It was in late December that the East German television station broadcast the news that Heike and Monty were to begin their now officially approved project to organise the painting of a piece of the Wall on East German territory. As Heike felt that the 1.3km stretch of Wall on Mühlenstrasse was too short for what she envisioned she decided to withdraw from the project.

Monty

Dave Monty (Siegfried Schönfelder)

I was born in Hessen on 15th February 1949 and attended a Swiss boarding school before coming to Berlin at the age of 16 in 1965.

Monty

I began studies in Law and Business Management neither of which I finished. I never had any interest in gaining diplomas or certificates I just wanted to learn the subject. I also studied Journalism for two years and am a self-taught artist.

The meetings I had with GDR officials to finalise arrangements for the gallery could make you anxious. It was my intention to have international artists. I was from the West and they had lots of artists in the East. I said we wouldn't have success unless we had international artists. The Stasi were clueless and I told them that, they then whispered to each other and I thought, "I won't get anywhere now." They knew however that I had the best arguments.

The first person in a commanding position with whom I came into contact was Lieutenant Colonel Menzel of the Border Guards. That was in winter 1989 and I had to talk to Menzel about the technicalities involved such as having artists cross from West to East on a regular basis. (The opening of the Wall on 9th November1989 didn't mean that all controls immediately stopped). Lt. Col. Menzel had the permission of Admiral Hoffman of the National Defence Ministry and General Steurich, who signed the letter giving permission for me to proceed, was Hoffman's representative.

Monty

There is one incident which happened at the beginning of the East Side Gallery project and I have never told the story before: I was approached by an artist from the GDR whose father was a Major and of course Stasi. I rejected her, didn't want to give her a space to paint. She then threatened me that her father was in the Stasi and when she couldn't paint her father was privileged etc. Then all of a sudden police appeared in their Trabis when I was there and they drove past at walking pace every 20 minutes. That was at the beginning of 1990. I told her she should bring me another draft and she went on again about consequences from her father.... The increase in the police presence then became really obvious. I was asked by a member of the People's police if I thought what I was doing was right – was that about the artist? I could never be sure.

It wasn't clear if it (the gallery) would happen or not. They could say ok and then change their minds and because of that I called a press conference on 29th January 1990, held in the Press Centre in East Berlin. Making it public meant it wouldn't have been so easy for them to go back on their word. I only got the written permission in February 1990.

My idea was that all the artists came out of the darkness, and that is what I have achieved.

It is my wish that the East Side Gallery will remain.

East Berlin no stranger

Christine's story

East Berlin was of course no stranger to me, having spent four years there in the employ of the British Embassy.

Monty's negotiations now successful, he contacted the two Artists associations (east and west) to ask them whether any of their members were interested in painting on the Berlin Wall. As Monty related, negotiations for permission to use the Wall on the Mühlenstrasse involved contact with the Stasi, there was no way round that. The Stasi were in the base fabric of the Society, their threads being the most predominant and strongest.

The East Side Gallery had very modest beginnings. I bought the first pots of paint and a few brushes and some artists bought their own tools and paint. A friend gave me an old ladder which I locked to the railings at the border when work was finished for the day and I brought my own ladder, transporting it on the roof-rack of my car. My old BMW car, Carolina, as my friend Rita named it, was the storage place for the paints and brushes used by the first few artists. It was also a place to sit out of the bitterly cold wind which whistled along the length of the Gallery until spring.

Monty was to seek sponsors for the project whilst my main task was to co-ordinate the artists' work. This required assisting them in any way necessary to complete their painting of the Wall be it transporting them to or from the airport, ferrying them across the border, buying or transporting paint and tools or any other tasks which arose.

The first artists

The First Artist

Narendra Jain. Photo Andreas Kämper

The first East Side Gallery artist was Dr Phil Narendra Jain (India) who was living in Berlin at that time, having lived and worked in Germany since 1967.

At the very beginning of the Gallery there was originally an image of the Statue of Liberty holding the Brandenburg Gate by the German artist Oskar which was copied onto the Wall by the American Artist Lance Keller. Oskar himself never painted on the Gallery, he simply gave permission for his image to be used. Lance Keller also painted the cover of Pink Floyd's record "The Wall" on the East Side Gallery. The original artist, Gerald Scarfe gave permission for this image to be painted once so that subsequent paintings by others have actually been done without Gerald's permission. Lance was a friend of mine and a brilliant copyist. He was kept very busy at that time painting murals on the walls of many Indian restaurants in West Berlin.

All the artists worked under difficult conditions but it was absolutely freezing in January 1990 when the first brushstrokes were applied and it often felt like being in a wind tunnel. Mühlenstrasse is like a race track and being a main road out of the centre of East Berlin it was always busy. Only a few artists painted at any one time. In the height of things there was probably a maximum of twelve working at the same time. We didn't have any meeting place other than on the street at the Gallery although my flat did function as an office at times.

There was no shelter apart from my car which was a welcome refuge from the elements. I often took a flask of tea with me so the warm drink was really appreciated. There was no water supply available apart from in the Guards building, and the artists had to go back and forth there to collect water with which to mix paint and clean their brushes. That wasn't so bad for the first artists who began painting near the Guards building but it became quite a trek for those who were working some distance from it.

As the Oberbaum bridge was still sealed off, we couldn't just nip across the bridge to a café to grab a coffee or bite to eat. Unlike now, there were absolutely no cafes or snack bars near us in the former East.

The first artists were men so they crossed the street and peed in the bushes when the need arose. When the first woman painter arrived (Kikue Miyatake) the border officials also allowed the artists to use their toilet.

The first artists

It soon became clear that Monty wasn't having much success getting anyone to give him money for the project. Monty liked a drink which may have resulted in possible sponsors being reluctant to engage with him. There was also no indication of how long this or any piece of the Wall would remain in situ which may have deterred potential sponsors. It was a time of great change.

At some point, in March 1990, Monty lost interest in the project. There was nothing said, no written statement, we just kind of drifted apart. I don't know how I imagined things were going to proceed when I was left alone in charge of 1.3km of the Berlin Wall. I was so wrapped up in the project that the idea of giving up never entered my field of thought. Monty did try to regain the project in late summer but by that time it was too late.

That was probably what you would call a pivotal moment in the East Side Gallery. With hindsight, I could have followed Monty and walked away at that point and saved myself a lot of stress and heartache and the East Side Gallery would have been a short-lived project.

Monty had never paid me a penny since I started working with him because he didn't have any money. I had been so enthralled by the whole idea that I never thought about getting a written contract from him. During the initial months of the East Side Gallery I earned a little money working for Peter Unsicker at Wall-StreetGallery in West Berlin assisting with his retrospective photo exhibition. Once East Side Gallery took off, I didn't have time to do both and gave up my position at Wall-StreetGallery.

The first artists

I suppose it was a bit surreal really to be simultaneously working on projects with the Berlin Wall in both East and West. It certainly was a strange situation I found myself in. I very quickly get bored with routine and for that reason have probably always sought adventure whether consciously or not. I have a tendency to just jump into things I find interesting without thinking about where they are going or worrying about any possible consequences. There was nothing boring or routine about the creation of the East Side Gallery.

The arrival of wuva

A member of wuva (werbeundveranstaltungsagentur) a newly established East German event and advertising company and concert promoter approached me in April 1990 with unsettling news. Wuva had obtained the exclusive rights (as of 1st March 1990) to advertise on the entire stretch of the Wall at Mühlenstrasse. What now I asked myself?

Although there were few completed paintings at that point, I suspect Rainer Uhlmann, the Managing Director of wuva and his team felt that on reflection using the Berlin Wall to advertise cigarettes and the like was rather controversial and wouldn't win them any friends. So after we met a couple of times wuva and I decided to join forces to finish the East Side Gallery. This meant that I was now employed and had a regular income. Wuva's advertising plans for the Wall along with any prospective income from it went out the window.

The East Side Gallery wouldn't of course exist without artists and their paintings. If however Rainer Uhlmann and I hadn't reached an agreement, then the artists would not have had the opportunity to continue. Wuva had the contract and was perfectly within its rights to use the Wall for advertising as planned.

The partnership entered into by wuva and I led to the completion of the East Side Gallery. There were many East/West Joint ventures starting up after the Wall opened and this was another, with me being from the West and wuva being an East German company. I continued my work looking after the artists but now I had help from wuva employees when needed.

The arrival of wuva

Rainer Uhlmann, and his team took care of the bureaucratic side and I was happy about that. Dealing with German bureaucracy is enough of a nightmare for Germans but for a foreigner it would drive you nuts. Now of course in addition to the bureaucracy of the West there was also the East German bureaucracy. You really needed to have an East German mentality to cope with that. The East Germans were so used to the way people were coerced and controlled that they knew how to work the system. I wouldn't have had a clue. Anyway, the interaction with the people whether artists, passersby or the media was the aspect of the job I enjoyed the most. I wasn't interested in spending time in boring meetings where people waffled on for hours without coming to any decision or conclusion. Rainer Uhlmann once said of me "you will never get Christine to do anything she isn't interested in." Well observed!

Bureaucracy was a particular nightmare with regard to the contract for the East Side Gallery. When wuva came along with their contract it seemed as though two separate parties had rights over the same stretch of Wall but that obviously wasn't the case. Monty had been given written permission to paint the Wall from the Ministry for National Defence in a letter dated 7th February 1990 but hadn't pursued a contract with the *Magistrat* as instructed to do so in the above mentioned letter.

The Border Guards as part of the Ministry of Defence had been the custodians of the Wall. With the gradual removal of the Wall those Guards were soon to be redundant although they would be kept busy for a few months dismantling the border.

The arrival of wuva

The authority over the remaining Wall passed to Friedrichshain Council as the Gallery stands in what was then the district of Friedrichshain. The signatory of the letter from the GDR Ministry, Major General Steurich, would have been aware of the imminent changes in Authority which is why in his letter of permission to Monty he recommended that contractual arrangements be clarified with the *Magistrat.* The district of Kreuzberg on the former west side of the Oberbaum Bridge has since merged its administration with Friedrichshain to form the joint Council of Friedrichshain-Kreuzberg.

Wuva's decision to no longer use the Wall for advertising meant that their original contract was invalid. The creation of an art gallery instead of a wall of advertising was a dramatic change of use which required wuva to alter the contract. Wuva started this procedure with Friedrichshain Council in April 90 and submitted a draft contract which was altered five times at the request of Friedrichshain Council; a new contract was never signed. Throughout the entire negotiations Friedrichshain Council acted as though they were the Legal Representative for this section of the Wall although this only became the case on 5th September 1990. They unilaterally cancelled the original contract with wuva on 17th December 1990. The letter was signed by the then Mayor of Friedrichshain district, Helios Mendiburu.

By the end of spring the Gallery took on a momentum of its own. Thanks to a donation from an East German company we now had sufficient paint to finish the Wall and the number of artists eager to participate in the project was steadily increasing.

The arrival of wuva

The media interest contributed to this as the project was reported worldwide and caught the attention of artists in other countries. We bought an old circus wagon in which to store the painting materials and parked it on the pavement in front of the Gallery (my car could no longer cope).

Regular drivers along this route had probably taken the uniform grey Wall for granted and no longer noticed it. This soon changed sometimes preceded by a bump. The large, bright murals were a distraction and several accidents happened as the driver's focus turned from the road in front to the art on the Wall. Fortunately none of the accidents were serious and as far as I am aware, nobody was injured.

There were four elements in the creation of the East Side Gallery, The first was Monty, the second, the author, the third wuva and the fourth the Artists. All of these elements were fundamental for the creation of the East Side Gallery, the first three being the most important. Some artists may argue that they were the most important element and of course there would be no Gallery without artists but without Monty, myself and wuva they would not have had the organisation and finance required to create such a gallery.

Any artist could then of course have painted on this stretch of Wall but their paintings wouldn't have lasted long as very soon someone else would have come along and painted over their work, exactly as happened with artwork on the Wall in West Berlin. So, the uniqueness of the East Side Gallery, the very fact that it was organised and financed as a collective project from start to finish is the reason it is still standing. If it hadn't been the organised project it was and artists came and went as was the case in West Berlin then this stretch of Wall would have been removed in 1990, that's a certainty. It's fortunate that wuva had the foresight to recognise the need to have East Side Gallery declared a protected monument.

A few people have airbrushed Monty out of the history of the East Side Gallery over the past 29 years. Without a beginning there can be no middle or end and Monty was the beginning. He deserves to be recognised for that.

Monty was awarded a Medal and certificate from Friedrichshain-Kreuzberg District Council on 18th February 2016, the "Bezirksmedaille des Bezirkes Friedrichshain von Berlin" (Friedrichshain District Medal). This was 26 years after Monty brought the East Side Gallery into being.

In 2011 Kani Alavi, the chair of the Artists Initiative was awarded the Bundesverdientskreuz (Federal German Cross of Merit) for, among other things, the creation of East Side Gallery – Kani Alavi's contribution to the creation of the East Side Gallery was the same as every other artist who took part in the project - he painted a picture.

Anyone who wanted to was able to paint on the East Side Gallery once they had signed a contract with the organiser, you didn't have to be a career artist. If *you* had been there at that time then theoretically you could have painted on the Wall as well. As Monty had made the Artists Associations aware of the project in late 1989, it turned out that the majority of those who took part were career artists. Soon artists eager to take part in the project arrived from other countries as word spread and the Gallery became known worldwide.

The arrival of wuva

As the Wall was completely exposed anyone could come along and paint or spray over existing paintings. To counter this, we had a team from wuva which patrolled the Gallery from early summer 1990 and any graffiti or paintings not created by an artist under contract were painted over This clean-up usually took place at night. It also prevented people from taking up spaces which had already been allocated to artists. The graffiti wasn't such a big issue in the early days of the Gallery; it became steadily worse as the Wall elsewhere disappeared.

The work of the artists wasn't censored or selected. There was no judgement of the artist's work although I can understand how this impression might have arisen. Monty had requested a sketch from each artist so that as far as possible similar styles weren't placed next to each other, not for any other reason. I continued with that process after Monty left. There was only one occasion when a member of wuva, Matthias Kleiber and I asked an artist to change a painting because we felt it just didn't fit with the overall theme. Otherwise the artists had complete control over what they painted. They were all under contract to wuva which technically gave wuva, as gallery owner, the authority to instruct the artists what to paint but that didn't happen.

*Magistrat. The Magistrat was the East Berlin equivalent of the West Berlin Senate. It had superior authority over the individual district offices. The seat of the Magistrat was in the Red Town Hall, where the Senate Chancellery is now located. Berlin is a city state and like other city states - Hamburg, Bremen, has a Senate.

What budget?

It may seem as though given the scale and significance of the East Side Gallery that there was a grand, detailed plan to create it and a budget to go with it. That was definitely not the case. When you consider the extraordinary historical and cultural importance of the East Side Gallery it is probably difficult to believe that it was created on a shoestring. It was a project which developed and unfolded as the year went on.

In many ways it mirrored what was happening in Berlin itself. There had been no rough plan or detailed blueprint for the practicalities involved in uniting Germany (at least none that you and I would be party to) so the creation of the East Side Gallery was similar to everyday life in that decisions were made on the hoof, on a daily or weekly basis with the facts on hand at that time and then as facts and situations changed plans were altered to suit.

None of us knew where the ESG was heading it wasn't a well-trodden path, just like reunification. You just went with the flow. We had no money and only sheer enthusiasm to keep us going.

Sponsorship from the following was a great boost:
Expo Tech, Köln/ Farben Günther, Berlin/
Geithainer Agrargenossenschaft e.G/Lacufa AG Berlin/ Luigi – Import/ Ostmühlen Ltd Berlin/ Sikkens/Staatsoper Berlin/
Herr K Lausch

CONTRIBUTORS

East Side Gallery Artists

East Side Gallery Photographer

Werner Heck,
Local Councillor for the Green Party
in Friedrichshain-Kreuzberg

Andreas Kämper

(Germany)

Photo: Jens Hübner

How I got to the "East Side"

It was a sunny weekday in May 1990. When you walked from the Oberbaum bridge along the Mühlenstrasse towards Ostbahnhof you could see on the River Spree side how the 3m high concrete Wall had been drawn into everyday life in the re-united city. Not even a year previously it had been strongly guarded as a *"hinterland wall" and no civilian could hang about here without punishment. Now the once monotone grey was decorated with graffiti, election posters and other statements. Since October 1989 I had been going out and about seeking photos for my photo diary.

Andreas Kämper

Here I came across Christine MacLean, the Manager of the East Side Gallery who saw to it that there was a creative working atmosphere onsite. Fulvio Pinna, the Italian, sat in his painting chair and was open for every fun distraction. Kikue Miyatake, a Japanese artist was scraping the remains of election posters from the area she wanted to paint on and the Frenchwoman, Muriel Raoux was engrossed in the completion of her work. What a relaxed fun scene it was there.

Soon after that I put my own picture on the grey concrete Wall and by autumn the 1.3km long stretch was filled with the most diverse images. It was really satisfying to see how this place of one time division and fear was filled with joyful and inspiring life which was embraced and reflected upon by passersby. The colourful and interesting facade became more and more known and slowly developed into a landmark of the Berlin metropolis, a sort of pilgrimage destination for both local and international tourists.

In 1996 an Artists Initiative East Side Gallery was formed and from that point on a commercialisation of the gallery could be felt. After that I had no direct experience of how the gallery developed.

I received no notification the first time the paintings were repaired in 2000 so that I was unable to renew my picture. Instead, Kani Alavi, the chairman of the Artists Initiative painted over it without my authorisation and made a very dilettantish copy. I would have been glad to have had the opportunity to recreate my original picture.

Andreas Kämper

A similar situation happened in 2009. The Senate made money available to completely restructure the gallery to maintain it for the city. Once again I was not notified and was presented with a fait accompli. The money made available had been spent and a subsequent improvement of my picture was no longer possible. I initiated a "crisis" meeting with those concerned (the Mayor, representative of S.T.E.R.N. Ltd and Kani Alavi) which was held in the Mayor's office. The Mayor admitted the validity of my claim but it was too late for my picture.

Despite all the current calamities in the surrounding area, I hope that in the future, through the existence of the East Side Gallery something of the optimistic mood and the pioneering spirit of the "turning point" will be retained.

*Hinterland Wall – parts of the Berlin Wall which weren't situated on the actual border but rather set back from it in the East. Sometimes there was another Wall when viewed from the East beyond the hinterland Wall. At the East Side Gallery the border was at the edge of the river on the west bank where it was impossible to build a Wall.

Andreas Kämper

Kikue Miyatake

(Japan)

I was born in Okayama, Japan, in 1954 and started painting as a child. I attended Chuo University in Tokyo and in 1979 I moved to New York, where I continued my studies of abstract painting and learnt new techniques such as silk painting, sculpture, and photography.

In 1985, while living in New York, I sold a painting to the wife of a New York lawyer. A German friend, who was visiting her, saw my painting and it was through her that I was introduced to the Frankfurt Gallerist Günter Steinmann.

Kikue Miyatake

In 1988 I had my first exhibition in Frankfurt, where I met the artist Günther Schäfer. I also visited West Berlin at that time. and took a day visa to visit East Berlin. I spoke to a lady there who said to me, "I don't know anything about the West." I was amazed at the contrast between West and East, as West Germany was free, no less than New York.

After the breaching of the Wall in 1989, Günther Schäfer came to visit me in New York. He said "Mr. Steinmann has reserved a segment of the Wall for you, Kikue, and he wants to know if you would like to put a painting on it." I was very excited about this opportunity to paint on the Berlin Wall. I wanted to celebrate the arrival of peace and freedom through painting.

Shortly after that I flew to Frankfurt, where I met up with Mr. Steinmann and Günther Schäfer. I arrived in Berlin on the night of the ninth of May 1990, and Günther then introduced me to Christine MacLean, the East Side Gallery Manager. The next day I went to see the Wall. I was able to stay with Christine in her big apartment in the Yorckstrasse; it was a great help to have support from such a kind and warm person. Günther and some other artists from the East Side Gallery also stayed with Christine while working on their paintings. Christine and I had some fun times together and we have been friends ever since.

In September 1991, twelve paintings on the East Side Gallery were damaged by a mentally disturbed man. My painting was one of them. Half of it was covered with green paint. I was very hurt by this. I flew from New York at my own expense and repaired my painting.

Kikue Miyatake

I returned to Japan in 1993 and have been living and working here ever since.

In 1996 permission was given by the Lower Historic Monument Authority in Berlin for my painting to be removed to make space for a driveway to the dance club in the Old Granary. The Wall pieces with my painting were removed and reinstalled at the side of the Granary. The next time I saw my painting it was completely covered in graffiti. I was really upset by this.

When, in 2009, an officially sponsored renovation made it possible, I put all my soul into recreating the painting. I was happy that the East Side Gallery was designated a Historic Monument and painting there was really a precious experience, which led to more exhibitions in Berlin, in particular during the run-up to the celebration of 150 years of Japanese-German relations, which provided me with further opportunities to meet many German people.

The whole East Side Gallery has to struggle with graffiti all the time but because my piece is now behind the Wall it is much easier to destroy. In 2014, the 25th anniversary of the demise of the Wall, my painting was again covered in terrible graffiti. I decided to write a letter to the Berlin Mayor. I wrote the letter in Japanese and sent it to the Japanese Ambassador in Berlin. It was translated into German there and then sent to the Berlin Mayor by special delivery. In my letter I told the mayor that I was very sad at the state of my painting which had become unrecognisable under layers of graffiti, despite the East Side Gallery being a historic monument. I also wrote that it wasn't just property damage, but a violation of the spirit and that I would like my picture to be restored to its original state and that my letter was an urgent entreaty that he consider the means and methods of how this might be achieved. I never received a reply.

I am very disappointed that my painting has been completely destroyed several times. I hope that now, since the East Side Gallery is being looked after by the Berlin Wall Trust, they will be able to do something about it. Maybe I will get the opportunity to paint it again.

For me it was a very exciting, meaningful experience to paint on the Berlin Wall. I am happy I had the opportunity to do it.

Kikue Miyatake

Margaret Hunter

(Scotland)

The Berlin Wall was still firmly in place when I arrived in the city to do post graduate study at the Hochschule der Künste following my Fine Art Degree at the Glasgow School of Art.

West Berlin at the time was a city of young people; it had an edgy creative atmosphere, decadence and subculture in the clubs alongside exhibitions, theatre, music and intellectual life. But that sense of freedom belied the concrete reality; no matter where you went in West Berlin you were always going to come up against the Wall and for many it impacted their life as a symbol of repression, restriction and resistance.

That all ended dramatically and unbelievably on the evening of 9th November 1989 when the Berlin Wall fell, heralding political reverberations in surrounding Eastern Bloc countries that eventually changed world politics.

A few months later I received a phone call from Christine MacLean, the woman responsible for organising a large group of artists to paint on the previously inaccessible east side of the Wall. This action represented a very precise moment of liberation.

I felt that it was a privilege to be invited. The project involved over 100 international artists from East and West; some were professionals, others, hobby artists and Berliners, all with something significant to say.

As the artists worked there was a tremendous jubilant atmosphere and camaraderie, interspersed with press interviews, television crews and kerb crawling buses full of tourists. But there were also those sudden moments of poignancy when we remembered the history of our *canvas* and the last young man from the East who died around 10 months before, trying to escape to the West.

My painting depicts two large mask-like heads lying side by side sometimes interpreted as 'strange bedfellows' They represent the two Germanys with dark lines and marks flowing dynamically between the two, suggesting interaction, ideas and exchange. I named my painting *Joint Venture* - buzzwords at that time.

In contrast to this *idealistic* view of German unification I painted *stitch* marks either side of the heads to attach rows of small figures, representing the situation for the *individual,* bending, pushing and contorting themselves to suit a new situation. This was for me the reality at that time, the fearful insecurity, as the familiar structures of life for every man, woman and child of the former GDR irrevocably and radically changed.

There was so much public interest in the East Side Gallery, as the longest stretch remaining of the Berlin Wall that it became a listed, protected monument. However during the following years its significance waxed and waned depending on political interests and despite the artists themselves sometimes renovating their murals many of the paintings became damaged by the elements and souvenir seeking tourists pecking out a piece of Wall history.

In 2009 the Berlin government funded its restructuring and renovation as a highlight event for the city's 20th anniversary of the Fall of the Wall and the artists, scattered around the world, were brought back to repaint their murals. There was an exhilarating atmosphere as the artists came together again after 20 years to participate in such a major, well-organised event. It was entirely at odds with our painting experience of 1990, when we had the bare materials and the few coveted ladders had to be shared along the Wall.

Today the East Side Gallery is on the tourist route in Berlin and attracts 3 million visitors annually. Despite this, in recent years there has been a development boom in the area and in 2013 a huge public outcry and organised protests failed to stop a large part of the Wall being taken down to make space for an access road to new luxury flats. It seemed that the days of the East Side Gallery, this unique, world renowned historical monument were numbered and its heritage status was no protection against political intrigue and the vested interests of property speculators

However more recently the East Side Gallery has come under the umbrella of the *Stiftung Berliner Mauer*, a government funded foundation entrusted with the preservation and care of the monument. There are plans for an information centre to be established with displays explaining the history and significance of the site, which will enhance its reputation and place in history.

The East Side Gallery has accompanied my life since 1990 and now at long last its safety seems assured. This is a huge relief that reassures and heartens me as one of the artists.

Margaret Hunter

photo of Margaret Hunter at work on 'Joint Venture'
attributed (copyright) to 'Rex Features'

Mary Mackey and George Denavit
In front of 'Tolerance'

Kikue Miyatake
Paradise out of the Darkness

Jim Avignon
Dooin it cool for the east side (II)

Mary Mackey

(USA)

<u>What brought me to Berlin?</u>

I had been living in London and decided that I needed to go to Berlin to see the Wall before it was removed. That was in the Spring of 1990. After my arrival in Berlin I met some people who persuaded me to stay, so I moved there.

<u>How did I get started with the ESG?</u>

In a magazine called *Prinz*, I came across an article about a project called the East Side Gallery and it said they were looking for artists to take part. I called up the number and found out the woman who was running the project spoke English and her name was Christine. She asked me to mark up a picture of what it was I wanted to paint on the Wall.

<u>How did I come up with the piece that I did and the name?</u>

I was really nervous, because I didn't consider myself to be much of a painter. I had done some painting but mainly just print making. At first, I enlisted a friend of mine to help me with it and asked if he'd like to collaborate. As we had difficulties agreeing on what to paint and I was getting a bit nervous about taking too long, I just did a quick sketch. I wanted to make a statement. I had been thinking about some of the injustices, from the Turkish immigrants, to the East Berliners, and so on. I found that sometimes the West Germans were a bit hard on outsiders or people who weren't as sophisticated as themselves. So my piece is called *Tolerance*, which is defined as: The ability or willingness to tolerate something, in particular the existence of options or behaviour that one does not necessarily agree with. The Motif is of two faces, one woman and one man, one black/brown and one white, facing away from each other frowning and then the two are facing each other smiling. It's very simple and maybe a bit too simple but as I've come to find out through the years it was relevant then and still is now.

What did the piece mean in 1990 and what does it mean now?

I thought then and I do now, especially with what's happening in the US at this time that we need more tolerance, not less, towards people who need help from other countries.

What did I want to get accomplished with the ESG?

After getting my painting done, I started to work selling the few postcards and tee-shirts that they had in a small kiosk at the beginning of the Wall. I started to think about using the photographs that I took to produce better tee-shirts, postcards, etc, so I asked my roommate if he wanted to get involved and he did. We went to the bank and borrowed 50,000 DM to start our business. I designed all the posters and tee-shirts and so on, and when we got ready to market them we hired people to sell all over the city. It was all a big blur of activity and things got lost, stolen, etc.

My partner and I unfortunately also had some difficulties and we split up. That was kind of a low point for me in Berlin as I lost both my residence and business at the same time.

After that I went to work as a photographer for an East German modelling agency. A few months later I returned to Denver having been away for two and a half years.

Mary Mackey

What was it like to work in an open space like that?

Back in 1990 we had no help with the painting. Christine gave me a key to a small caravan containing old donated paint that had been sitting in the hot sun all summer. My contribution, since it was one of the later pieces, was quite a ways down the Wall from the beginning. I would have to take about three trips to get a ladder and all the equipment to paint it. The East Side Gallery is on a very busy street and back then there were still a lot of 2 stroke engine cars that put out a tremendous amount of pollution, so not only was it hot but very stinky as well. The ladder I used was only so high and I could only reach so far up so the area at the top was not painted. When I came back in 2009 they had scaffolding and I could reach the top, but decided to try and replicate it to be as original as possible.

How was re-painting your piece in 2009?

When I arrived to re-paint my contribution it was a completely different experience. For one thing they had a tent where all the artists would meet and then get help from all the wonderful volunteers who helped you pick out the supplies, such as paints and anything else you might need. Another big and added surprise was getting to meet some of the artists that I never got to see the first time around. In 2009 as well as 1990 not everyone was there at the same time. I met a few people in 1990 and then a lot more in 2009.

One of the first things I noticed about my piece was they had done a lot of repairs to the Wall itself which meant that really most of my painting was gone. Secondly, ten years before some people tried to get hold of me but I did not have an email address back in 1999 so someone had repainted my work because the graffiti was so bad that you could hardly see the painting anymore. They had done an ok job, and I was one of the lucky ones to have someone try to redo my work, because by then most of the East Side Gallery was unrecognizable.

When I got back in 2009 I just decided to paint the area white and start over again. With this beautiful blank canvas available to me I decided to create a composition that represented more of my painting style in 2009 and then paint over it and redo my original artwork from 1990. For this alternative piece I wanted to do something abstract because that was how my style had developed, so I did and took many photos of this work, which I dedicated to the people of Denver Colorado.

Back in 1990 I had been very embarrassed about my original design. For one I realised that I had been very influenced by Thierry Noir's piece which had faces with big eyes and big lips. I felt I should have come up with something original. After being back in Berlin for a month however, talking to people about the whole thing and talking to Thierry as well, I came to realise that mine meant something different from his and he was not offended by the similarity. Now ten years later I'm more and more pleased with what I've done because of the relevance of the meaning. I get quite a few people looking me up and wanting to talk about my mural and about Tolerance.

Why didn't I leave the new painting and repaint the original one?

The reason that I did not leave that abstract painting on there was because they wanted me to repaint it just the way it was in

1990 and I'm glad now because it represents that time and still has relevance today.

<u>What was Berlin like for me in 1990, 2009 and the last time we were in Berlin in 2015?</u>

It seems as though when I look back to 1990 I was young and free to do what I wanted. I moved around at will and did whatever it took to make money, by cleaning houses in London then selling beer and water off the back of my bike in Berlin. By 2009 I was running a gallery back in Denver, had bought a house and settled down in my life as an artist. Going back to Berlin was always a big dream for me. I had not been back to Berlin since 1990. So in 2009 the city had changed to something I did not recognise. The West was very much the same but the East had changed so much. I was worried that when I would go back after 20 years that I could not find that spark that I found the first time. But I just found a different spark and truly enjoyed myself for the month I was there. Consequently I've been able to return four more times in six years.

Still I miss Berlin I'll always have a place in my heart for the city and the culture. In 2013 I got married to George and was able to travel again and enjoy a new and fabulous relationship. We have enjoyed going back to Europe and travelling together and I showed George around Berlin where he met my friends from the East Side Gallery.

Mary Mackey

<u>How do I feel about approval being granted to build a hotel right behind the East Side Gallery?</u>

I had always wished that they would do more of a museum than a hotel or condos or some kind of development. I thought with all the money and everyone knowing that The East Side Gallery is so famous and has about a million visitors a year that the government would be interested in preserving that whole area.

<u>Being a photographer how did that affect my painting and what did I want out of photographing all the art and what happened to all of those pictures?</u>

The art was the most important thing to me at the time and what took me to Berlin in the first place was photography. It wasn't only the historical part but then getting involved with the ESG. I asked Christine if I could be the official photographer of the ESG and she said yes. Really neither one of us really knew what that entailed but I just wanted to know that I could take photos of all the work and put them on tee shirts, posters, postcards and so on. I did that with the help of my roommate Hilde Lehmann. We saw an opportunity to get involved with all aspects of the ESG. I also wanted to get to photograph everything for a record for myself and any news agency. I knew that this project was truly amazing and important.

Before I left Berlin I rented a really good 2 ¼ film camera and used all of my money to buy film. I went around the whole city and did a documentary called a day in the life of Berlin. I stayed up all night and day and had a friend help record each of the photos. It was too bad that after I got back to Denver and started my Gallery in less than a year the basement where I had put all of the negatives and photos got flooded. I had lost almost everything I had worked really hard for. I was able to save some and make some reproductions of them.

How has being involved with the ESG changed or influenced my work or life?

Well there is the saying from Andy Warhol "everyone in the future will have 15 minutes of fame" and I feel I had not only 15 minutes but many more because of the ESG. I think that it has proven to me that working at trying to be in the right place at the right time, getting yourself out there in the world and participating, risking, challenging, and going beyond your comfort zone can put you in the right place at the right time. I don't think that I would ever have had the courage to open my own art gallery without doing what I did in Berlin.

Mary Mackey

Rosemarie Schinzler

(Germany)

How I came to paint at the East Side Gallery Berlin in 1990

I had visited East Berlin several times with my husband years before the Fall of the Wall. He gave lectures there which were "forbidden" in the context of his professional activity as a professor for social pedagogy. Whilst he was busy lecturing I explored the East part of the city, in particular the Pergamon Museum.

When the Wall fell on November 9th 1989 we knew we would soon be taking a trip to East Germany with our children. We were eager for them to see and experience this border situation with their own eyes.

Rosemarie Schinzler

That was when I discovered at the Oberbaumbrücke what we now know as the East Side Gallery. I was fascinated by the idea of changing this frightening, grey, 3.45m high wall and borrowed paint from one of the artists who was there to paint a small picture as a Berlin souvenir.

Then someone in a passing car stopped and pointed out to me that my picture would soon be painted over because the space had already been allocated. At the same time I was given an address where I could apply to paint a section.

During the journey home to Freiburg my family and I developed the first ideas and sketches on the given topics - environment, peace and freedom. My picture "Let It Grow" symbolises the beginning of a new era. It stands for the growing together of East and West. It was important to me that a real plant grew out of the wall of terror. The title "Let It Grow" was inspired by Willy Brandt's great speech to end the division of the city and the country. "What belongs together grows together."

In June 1990 I started on my piece "Let it Grow". This picture was hard work. Although I had practised working with concrete before, the material did not want to bond with the Wall. The heat, noise and stink on the six-lane street added to the difficulties of working there. The traffic was chaotic due to the many construction sites. On one of my first days there I met Christine MacLean to sign the contract. The advertising company wuva had acquired the rights to market the pictures for five years.

Rosemarie Schinzler

Let it Grow

Everything Open

Rosemarie Schinzler

I met with Christine MacLean in front of my finished picture. But now that there was a gap between my picture and the previous one Christine asked me if I was willing to paint another picture. I asked for time to think about it but soon afterwards the idea for the second picture "Everything Open" developed in my head.

My second painting originated in Berlin and was inspired by Picasso's Peace Doves and the Brandenburg Gate. In September 1990 for the opening ceremony of the ESG I found my picture "Everything Open" on the cover of the *Berliner Morgenpost*. The chief editor said that this picture had caught the mood of the people. Over the last 30 years

I have been to the ESG several times to repair my paintings. When in 2009 I repainted both, Gernot Erler a member of the German Parliament visited me at the Wall and supported my work at the ESG which was very encouraging.

In a conversation with Dr. h. c. Gernot Erler (1) on 29 October 2014 in his SPD office in Freiburg on the topic "Between Euphoria and Horror: Everything Open?" he explained,

"What fascinated me about your work was the idea of peace, which is expressed through visual language. We had always hoped that the Fall of the Berlin Wall would be a symbol that the time of bloc thinking, of the Cold War, was over and that a European Peace Order would become possible...Now especially we are in a situation in which this hope for a new European Peace Order is called into question...

Your images, which basically symbolise this hope for peace, have once again taken on an unwelcome relevance, because suddenly things we believed to be a certainty have shifted and are now being questioned. Thus your picture "Everything Open" suddenly becomes topical in a completely unexpected way. We are being warned and reminded that in 1989, 25 years ago, "Everything Open" was associated with expectations of a very positive kind."

The Wall was a symbol of a lack of openness. Today people are frightened by this saying, "Everything Open" because at the moment under certain circumstances it is actually open to a possible unavoidable return to the relationships of the Cold War... and as far as the Wall itself is concerned, I am glad that substantial parts still remain.

There is still this great "East Side Gallery," which, even if it is painted over and can no longer be seen in its original state, still shows what the artists' thoughts and reactions to the Fall of the Wall were back then. It is a very vivid visual teaching. It is also a minor substitute for what the new generation can no longer experience personally. That's why I'm passionate that this Wall doesn't disappear completely. We need it for a culture of remembrance for a new generation."

(1)Dr. h. c. Gernot Erler, Member of the German Parliament, former Minister of State, Coordinator for Russia, Central Asia and the Eastern Partnership Countries.

Rosemarie Schinzler

Sabine Kunz

(Germany)

Photo: Ringela Riemke

I was born in Zwickau in Saxony and started painting as a child. My mother encouraged and motivated me and when I was 12 or 13 years old she arranged for me to attend weekly drawing classes at the Martin Hoop factory with the most important contemporary painter in Zwickau, Karl-Heinz Jakob. My first artistic steps were also encouraged by my brother-in-law Uwe Bullmann and my cousin Brigida Böttcher, both painters.

In the summer of 1970 I received a letter advising me that my promised place in Halle (Saale) at the Burg Giebichenstein College of Art to study art and tapestry design had been withdrawn. The wording was as follows: "Due to the multiple applications by Sabine Kunz at the Fachhochschule

Schneeberg, at the Kunsthochschule Berlin Weissensee and at the Burg Giebichenstein in Halle we are withdrawing her student place because multiple applications are not allowed in the GDR."

My mother phoned the Principal of the department which dealt with Students' issues at the University in Halle to arrange an interview with one of the professors. She explained to the professor how important these studies were for me and that she couldn't understand how anyone could obstruct a young person's progress in this way. Then there was the irritating question of how the University Department knew that I had successfully passed the other aptitude tests?

The professor tried to justify himself and asked me what my plan was and what had been agreed with my future lecturer, Inge Götze. I told him that I wanted to do a two-year internship at the textile manufacturers as preparation for my art studies and that my university place was secured from her side. I also told him that we would spend a week in the preliminary internship sketching and plan a week of practical work in the tapestry factory. He listened to me and I was very nervous about his answer. It was: "I allow you to do a 'trial' year and if I don't 'hear' about you during this year, you can study with us." This restrained threat meant for me to behave "well." I accepted, glad that I had not been deprived of my place at university. I felt inwardly humiliated and went into the first year of my internship, determined not to make any "mistakes."

So at the age of 19, shortly before my 20th birthday I was at the castle Giebichenstein in Halle. For the first two years I studied drawing and weaving.

The Fall of the Wall happened at the same time I received my diploma. I was so absorbed in my diploma thesis at the art academy however, that I didn't notice much of the prelude to the opening of the Wall. The Wall was still in my head. When my professor told me that the Berlin Wall was being painted and that the students could apply to take part, I quickly made a sketch.

And so at the beginning of June 1990 I went to Berlin to work on my painting after successfully passing my diploma. In the end still not really awakened from the GDR sleep. I took in the situation on the ground and parked my Trabi opposite the Wall. The volume of traffic was very heavy at that time.

I was seized by a tremendous wave of emotion as I stood on the other side of the street in front of this huge Wall with the challenge to paint a picture. For me it was for eternity, that feeling. That is, I felt the historical challenge. I also felt the artistic challenge and the chance to create a great work. I understood that something new was about to begin; slowly step by step with new opportunities but also with limitations.

I had previously only known the GDR and the other Eastern Bloc countries. I was seized by a strange euphoria at the sight of the Berlin Wall, this imaginary opening which illuminated this bleak street, - without having seen anything from the West. A feeling of symbolic freedom, the open sky the expanse over the Berlin Wall impressed me.

Here I was now standing at arm's length from the Berlin Wall next to me everything was free, just grey wall. A few artists were talking shop whilst scraping the posters off the Wall. I sensed impatience within me, an art degree course behind me, finally getting the chance to paint. I wanted to prove my artistic ability.

An old works caravan stood on the pavement where today there is a gap in the Wall and it was full of paint tubs. Someone handed out the paint. We stored the ladder there after the work on our painting was done for the day. Maybe I came across Christine MacLean there but I can't remember her. I can remember my neighbour who painted Erich Fried's quote and recall talking to her. She is already deceased.

Standing in front of the grey Wall, the busy road and my Trabi behind me, a watchtower to my side was the moment when a deep joyful feeling to be free slowly surfaced during the painting of my mural. This is expressed in my painting "The Dancers."

The nicest experience with the East Side Gallery, the largest open air gallery in the world, took place in September 1990. It was the successful official opening on a ship moored on the river Spree, in the presence of artists from all over the world who had spontaneously painted at the time. It was a very well attended event with members of the television, radio and press also present.

A nice catalogue of all the East Side Gallery artists' paintings was made. I keep a copy of it with my original sketch. I was a member of an ESG Artists' Initiative in 1994 although the registered association (e.V) wasn't founded until 1996.

At the end of 1999 Kani Alavi, the chairman of the Artists Initiative asked me to paint my Wall picture again on canvas of approx. 70 x 130 cm. This picture was to be shown in an exhibition in the Korean Embassy. The execution of this small second Wall picture was very difficult for me because I was heavily pregnant at the time. I was never paid for this painting and I never saw it again. Despite my requests and demands it was never returned to me. My experiences with the Artists Initiative were very ambivalent.

Due to a shoulder injury in 2009 I couldn't recreate my picture at the same time as everyone else but did so in 2010. My painting and the Berlin Wall have taken a real hold of me they continue to accompany me and my artistic career.

The Wall now has a dual purpose since reunification. Its role as a symbol of terror has been surmounted and replaced by a sense of joy and hope for the future keenly and eloquently expressed in the paintings of my colleagues. This contrast of past and present is invaluable and should be cherished by the city, never to be forgotten.

Culture and art are important for society. People are adopting a lifestyle which is increasingly aligned with computers and viewing habits with their resultant dependencies. The consequences for us and future generations will have to be dealt with by doctors. By promoting creative intuition and mastery of the fine arts, we can create a counterbalance with art and culture.

Sabine Kunz

In 2013 I attended a hearing to discuss the future of the East Side Gallery which was held at the Friedrichshain-Kreuzberg Museum in Berlin at which I presented my project idea for a sculpture park behind the gallery.

Maybe it was just a lovely illusion that freedom was to be found on the other side of the Wall. This freedom - commercial freedom - is now moving closer to the Wall. We have to admit to ourselves that commerce, as far as the design of the Spree side is concerned, was clearly faster and took advantage of the fact that those responsible were asleep. But despite the residential tower the new hotel block and other detractions the East Side Gallery will continue to be a place of interest to visitors from all over the world.

Sabine Kunz

Jim Avignon

(Germany)

How did you feel about painting the Wall, did you do that in
West Berlin?

What motivated you to participate in the ESG project?

I was new to the city and saw this as a good opportunity to
show my art to a wider audience.

How did you feel about painting the Wall, did you do that in
West Berlin?

No, never. I only moved to Berlin in '88 and just saw the Wall
as part of the annoying border controls.

When I painted the East Side, it was first and foremost for me a
painting surface like any other, just dirtier and bigger.

What was your overall experience of the project both in 1990
and since?

When we painted the Wall in 1990, a somewhat naive "we
artists make the world a better place" spirit floated over the
whole project. That quickly evaporated when I saw that a lot of
money was earned with the merchandise for ESG and the
artists went away empty-handed. I complained about it in 1991
during a TV interview in front of my picture and was then
threatened by the sellers in the ESG shop. That same night I
wrote the words money machine across my picture. It
remained like that until 1999.

Have you ever repaired or repainted your mural?

No, never. I find art on the street should appear and gradually
disappear or be painted over. I like it when the pictures are
fully tagged and people scratch their names into the picture.

Jim Avignon

The street is not a museum - when I paint something on the street I know one day someone will paint something over it.

How did you react when you were asked to repaint your picture in 2009?

I refused to restore my picture because it was a bit silly as a 40 year old to recreate a picture I had painted when I was 20. I suggested that my space on the Wall be given to another (young) artist – but that was rejected. I even suggested that friends could restore my mural (and earn some money from it). That was also rejected because only ESG Gallery artists are allowed to paint at ESG. What nonsense.

What motivated you to paint a completely new mural in 2013 and what was the general response?

For a long time I had been thinking about painting a new mural. In 2013 when the TV station *arte* asked me if I had an idea for a flash mob in Berlin - I knew immediately what I wanted to do. Together with a lot of helpers I was able to create a new painting on the ESG in no time at all. There was quite a lot of excitement, encouragement and protest - for a while it even looked as if I had to go to prison.

From your experience, is the copyright you have as an artist always respected? Examples?

There is no copyright covering art in a public space in Germany and I think that's a good thing. However, it is a different matter when only the painting is shown ie with no reference to the artist, often the case when ESG images are used for commercial purposes.

Jim Avignon

For my original image, I had ceded the rights to the East Side Gallery and was often annoyed about it. With the new image, I have already had a few interesting situations with Telekom, who used it for an advertising spot.

The Berlin Wall Foundation is now in charge of the East Side Gallery. Do you have any comments or opinion on that?

No

Any other comments you would like to make?

No

Jim Avignon

The Photographer - Rita May

(Germany)

I was born in Mühlbach (a small village near Chemnitz, East Germany) in 1948. I grew up surrounded by nature. I attended Primary and Secondary school in Naumburg/Saale. My afternoons were spent roller skating or ballet dancing. Later I took up gliding as a hobby. From 1968 to 1972 I studied Education at the High School in Erfurt specialising in German and Art.

I worked as a teacher in East Berlin for seven years. At the same time I attended courses in classical massage, pantomime and photography. It was difficult to get out of the teaching profession. It was totally different to the West where anyone could follow the career of their choice and it was easy to change jobs. Our Education was free and for that reason the

State determined where we were needed. If you had studied then you had to "work off your debt." If you wanted out you could hand in your notice but you didn't get your *cadre file. Without which no other company could employ you. I still risked it as I wanted to be self-employed.

The Stasi didn't like that as you couldn't be monitored so easily. So, it was a case of once a teacher always a teacher. On top of that, the State needed teachers. It was considered a matter of honour to support socialism in this way. Nevertheless because I held a licence for folk art as Head of a pantomime group in the "Pionierpalst", I got a tax number. It took three years (every year I presented my photography work) until I was awarded a licence for Journalism and photography. In 1986 I could finally work officially as a freelance photographer for the following clients: *Planetverlag* – Postcards/*Amiga* – record covers *Kunsthandel der DDR* – Posters/*Berliner Prater* and *Die Möve* as in-house photographer.

Publications: *NBI; Spiegel; Neues Deutschland; Der Morgen; Junge Welt; Evangelischer Kirchenkalender; Wochenpost; Magnus; Du und ich; Das Magazin; Der Hund.*

None of these publications existed after the "turning point" as the Fall of the Wall is referred to. *Das Magazin* went bankrupt and didn't pay outstanding fees and has reappeared under new management. *Der Planetverlag* disappeared with all the original photos I gave them.

I continued to try and earn a living as a photographer but it wasn't possible. After being unemployed for a short while I was employed under the Government job creation scheme at:

The Photographer - Rita May

Netzwerk/Spielkultur, Kinderring Berlin e.V., Spatzenkino, Menschenskinder e.V., Kreativhaus, Regenbogenhaus. During these years I gained more qualifications in theatre pedagogic, Reiki, Feldenkrais, Shiatsu and Reflexology. Today I work more in this sector and have chosen to live in the country in Prignitz, Brandenburg.

* cadre file was the file kept on you by your communist unit

<u>Five naked guys in Berlin</u>

The idea was born in a pub in Prenzlauer Berg. Naked men in a public space, a place which almost all (East) Berliners were familiar with. It was to be a poster for the East German art trade. I met the five friends who were prepared to be models in Dimitroffstrasse (now called Danziger Strasse) at 7.30am on a summer's day in 1986. We tested their walk and the camera setting. Then they quickly went into a close and undressed (in those days nobody locked the main entrance door). After a few minutes the photo was in the box. The fun was accompanied by a certain excitement If the police came then one of us was to leave with the camera and I would "take the blame." Soon after the image was available for the art trade but what do you know, the poster couldn't be distributed because on the rail bridge in the background hung an advertising banner for *Neues Deutschland* (*New Germany*, the newspaper which was the mouthpiece for the GDR Government). A political innuendo?

Then the Wall came down. In a special edition of *Zitty*, a West Berlin magazine, "Eating, Dancing and Drinking in East Berlin" the photo was a hit: *Neues Deutschland* (New Germany) took on a completely new meaning. At that time there was great interest on the part of the Media – *Spiegel*, *Stern*, Radio and Television, *Der Morgen*. Later the photo was used as a CD and book cover and exhibitions wanted to display it. Today it is available as a postcard in a few erotic shops. Thus you become known for a short while and soon after sink into anonymity again.

In the autumn of 1991 *Das Magazin* asked its readers to send in their private erotic photos. This magazine was really popular in the GDR and featured a nude picture every month. This is how the travelling exhibition "the Naked Republic" which toured Germany came about. One of the stops on the tour was the Erotic Museum in Hamburg where, without my permission, exhibition posters and postcards were printed and offered for sale. The museum operator didn't exactly volunteer my fee for "naked men." I realised then that this was "how capitalism functioned!" It happened many times that photo rights were evaded. Even the Newspaper *Neues Deutschland* copied my photo in an exhibition and then used it for one of its articles. All these experiences remind me of an interesting exciting time.

East Side Gallery

Through colleagues at the Berlin *Prater* (East Berlin Theatre) I received a contract from wuva in 1990 to photograph the creation of the "East Side Gallery." I was there several times a week with my Pentax camera (6 x 7) From May to September 1990. There was little time to get into conversation with the artists and I wasn't able to do portraits of all of them. It was really difficult to photograph the artworks because the camera distance couldn't always be accurately selected from the opposite side of the road. There was an almost constant stream of traffic with barely a minute between each vehicle. Sometimes friends accompanied me and gave me a signal when I needed to quickly jump off the road.

I was really enthusiastic about the project. I liked the informality of it. The international artists had a draft of their work, but no selection committee to deal with. I was fascinated by the energy of the images which emerged at a rapid pace, so different in style and emotional message.

When the job was finished, I got only half of the agreed fee together with a note "the rest later." That dragged on and after wuva's bankruptcy I was left with only 80 DM. The publication of the second edition of the Wall catalogue a little later and thus the recognition of my work was a slight consolation.

The Photographer - Rita May

I gave all my slides to wuva, the client, as agreed. Many years later therefore when asked "Do you still have photos of the East Side Gallery" my answer was, regrettably no."

I recall an episode which occurred a little later. I was asked to document the painting "Keep Entrance clear day and night" by Christos Koutsouras, which had been painted over. Next to me stood an inconspicuous young man, who said; "that space was free to paint wasn't it?" He hadn't recognised the work of art and had painted his somewhat tacky sunrise over the original.

Rita May

Werner Heck

Politics and the East Side Gallery.

A story by Werner Heck of neglect, ignorance, failure and also of resistance.

Werner, you are a local Councillor in the Friedrichshain-Kreuzberg Council, the local parliament in the Berlin district which was responsible for the East Side Gallery until its transfer to the Berlin Wall Foundation in November 2018. We would like to hear more from you about this.

Werner Heck

How is it possible that local Councillors and Berlin politics allowed the East Side Gallery, the longest remaining piece of the Berlin Wall and at the same time one of the outstanding symbols of the Fall of the Wall and the peaceful revolution of 1989 and as such one of the most visited monuments in Berlin, to be in such a wretched state on the 30th anniversary of the Fall of the Berlin Wall?

The East Side Gallery which is already surrounded by; the so-called entertainment district; the urban nightmare around the *Mercedes-Benz Arena* and the luxury residential tower *Living Levels* on the former death strip will soon be almost completely overshadowed and degraded to the function of a garden wall when a 120 metre long nine-storey block is built behind it!

I think the fundamental problem is that the Berlin Senate or rather those governing there have still not grasped what a unique legacy they have in the East Side Gallery, as recognised by the three million yearly visitors to it. At the same time, there have always been strong financial players and commercial interests that perceive the Wall and with it the East Side Gallery primarily as an obstacle to their exploitation of the former death strip as lucrative building land. For a long time, these interests were closely interlinked with the governing officials in Berlin, especially in the construction and real estate sectors. Also, the district Council, which was closest to it, never had sufficient resources for monument conservation, urban and financial development nor the political power to protect the East Side Gallery from the capitalist profit interests of the real estate lobby and the ignorance prevailing at State level: At least not to the extent necessary or with the result we would have liked. I will try to tell the story from our perspective. I'll concentrate above all on the impending degradation of the East Side Gallery to a garden wall for luxury living and how we got to that point. What will ultimately become of the "living monument" owned by the Berlin Wall Foundation is another story whose end is not yet in sight. Although I fear that a representative of the "Persecuted by the GDR regime" might ultimately be right when she said to me at our colloquium on the future of the East Side Gallery in October 2017:

"At this piece of the Wall, there is a repeat of the appropriation of our revolution by the West. What happens here is no longer decided by us but by the representatives of the victors of reunification. Their form of Wall remembrance reduces us to the role of victim and they are now even taking away the memory of our Utopia, which found its expression here. The opportunity to relate these ideas to our present by staging contemporary artistic events at this symbolic place is restricted by the erection of ever new walls but this time the intention is less to lock people in but rather to lock them out."

1991 - 1999 The first chapters

In November 1991 the East Side Gallery was placed under a conservation order. Without this decision the East Side Gallery would no longer exist. Everywhere in the city people wanted to get rid of the Wall as quickly as possible, this concrete reminder of the years of division. The newly reunited city was in Gold Rush mood. Many of the plots located at the Wall and on the former Death Strip were reclaimed. The plot at Mühlenstrasse 6063 was one of those returned to the original owner then sold on.

Werner Heck

In 1992, the Senate Department for Urban Development under Senator Volker Hassemer (CDU) commissioned an urban development competition called "Hauptbahnhof" (main station) (today Ostbahnhof - East station). The result: In addition to 10 "town houses" and a high-rise building a 120-metre-long block is to be built on the banks of the River Spree between Oberbaumbrücke and Schillingbrücke. The Wall itself, including the East Side Gallery, is seen as merely an obstacle to construction with the former death strip representing a lucrative building site. Initially none of this had any immediate impact on the East Side Gallery. Contrary to what some Berlin politicians had originally expected, there was no rush on the reunited city, at least not from financially strong investors willing to build and so the results of the competition remained at first urban planning ideas which did not necessitate any building legislation. This gave the East Side Gallery a few years of peace and quiet during which no one really cared much for it. Many paintings exposed to the weather, faded, disappeared, were painted over or covered by graffiti, while bars and clubs were set up on the wasteland of the former death strip.

In 1996 a player who is ultimately responsible for turning the ideas of the urban planning competition into actual building legislation enters the stage threatening the existence of the East Side Gallery: Peter Strieder. He was initially Mayor of Kreuzberg from 1992 to 1995. It didn't hurt his career when his SPD party lost the majority there. Not only that, as early as January 1996 he became Urban Development Senator under the incumbent Mayor, Eberhard Diepgen and remained so even after the break-up of the coalition which had governed to that point as a result of the banking crisis in Berlin in 2001 and the election of Klaus Wowereit as Governing Mayor. It was only in April 2004 that Strieder had to give up all political offices after he was put under investigation by the public prosecutor's office in connection with a scandal involving the building of the *Tempodrom*. The proceedings were dropped in 2007. However, even after his resignation, the former building senator is still involved in urban development today as a consultant to various real estate companies. He is regarded as the best networked person in Berlin's social democracy.

In my opinion 1999 was the year in which the course was set for what was to come. It was the year in which the relocation of parliament and government, which had been decided in 1991 took place and Berlin was no longer just the nominal capital but the real seat of government of the Federal Republic of Germany. This of course awakened great hopes among speculators and the real estate industry for which Peter Strieder created the preconditions. It was he who carried over the results of the, by that time, seven-year-old competition into the so-called "Planwerk Innenstadt" (inner city plan). This however changed this urban nightmare into planning law, with far-reaching consequences for the local Council because it is they who are actually responsible for drawing up development plans. They only become legally binding when the local parliament, approves them, unless the Berlin Senate, as a higher authority, takes over the planning because of a city-wide interest. This in a way is what has happened with the enactment of this plan. It is these legal and administrative procedures that ultimately determine the future of the East Side Gallery. The next step, which in turn will be taken by Senator Peter Strieder, will finally make them binding. Thus, the district must issue a joint preliminary building permit for the high-rise and the hotel block according to §34 BauGB on the basis of this inner city plan after Strieder had taken over the process because of "urgent city-wide interest." In the letter from Strieder's office, it stated that with regard to the East Side Gallery, "selected openings are to be made in the East Side Gallery within the scope of the building project." After a meeting with Senate Building Director Hans Stimman, the State Monument Office representative agreed. This means that construction can now take place at the East Side Gallery.

2001 - 2011 Two breakthroughs and one referendum

First of all nothing happens; first and foremost because the expected rush of investors to the capital doesn't materialise. With the merger of the Council districts in 2001, a new City Councillor for development, Franz Schulz takes office. He would later become the district Mayor. He ensures that the merged district Friedrichshain-Kreuzberg gradually buys up all the plots for the 10 "townhouses" in the competition result and tries to secure the entire site behind the East Side Gallery as a public park. The owners of the plots designated for the high-rise building and hotel block do not want to sell however. The results of these efforts will be laid down in a development plan (V-74) in order to permanently secure the areas previously designated for building land as green spaces. The remaining areas where the owners are not willing to sell are recorded with the building legislation existing at that time, already in effect with the issue of preliminary building permits in 2000. If the district had wanted to classify the areas where the owners were not willing to sell as green areas and thus restrict the existing building regulations, it would have had to prove at the time of the classification that the financing of the consequences of such a plan change (compensating owners) was assured. With figures in the upper millions, the State would have had to declare its willingness to make the necessary funds available to the district Council, since the local budgets provided by the State are not adequate for such purposes and the local Councils are therefore dependent on the State with regard to major investments or compensation payments. But Senator Strieder declared during the development plan procedure that the existing planning was sound and therefore the district would not receive a cent for a plan change that deviated from the previous building legislation. The purchase of the other areas, which today represent the East Side Park, could therefore only be financed by compensation payments from other construction projects. For example, the Mercedes-Benz Arena. In 2006, the largest breach to date with a length of 41 metres was made in the East Side Gallery for this arena. Visitors were to be given an uninterrupted view of the banks of the Spree and direct access to the pier, even though other plans by the Anschutz Entertainment Group to create a completely new quarter here were not implemented until much later.

As I said, at first it was simply the case that the initial expectations of large returns from concrete gold in the booming metropolis of Berlin were not realised. Instead, they bought and sold, bought, sold, bought, etc. The wastelands and open spaces were initially preserved irrespective of this roulette and green spaces were created. In July 2008, the initiative *Mediaspree versenken* (sink the Mediaspree- a movement to halt the construction on the banks of the Spree) was successful when 87 percent of the participating citizens voted in the peoples' referendum "*Spreeufer für alle*"(banks of the Spree for all). Key demands: No high-rise and an undeveloped 50-metre-wide riverbank. The result however was not binding. Nevertheless, a special committee is formed in September 2008 in which members of the various parliamentary groups and the citizens' movement *Mediaspree* discuss possible ways to change building plans in line with the public's decision. But at the end of February 2009 the Senate intervenes in the negotiations. It fears compensation claims from investors should development plans be changed and also has "serious reservations" about the abandonment of the high-rise building on the Elsen Bridge. It therefore threatens to deprive the district of its planning sovereignty. The Urban Development Senator, Ingeborg Junge-Reyer, has assured the investors of planning security. However, the local Mayor Franz Schulz continues to feel obligated to comply with the result of the peoples' referendum and attempts to implement it at every opportunity. Just such an opportunity for the East Side Gallery arises in the middle of 2012.

2012 Between hope and disappointment

In 2012 there was a realistic chance to prevent this construction and any development at the East Side Gallery. The 7-year planning guarantee deadline under the Building regulations for the two plots which the Council had been unable to purchase was to expire in August 2012. The district Council and local parliament wanted to seize this opportunity and initiate a development plan amendment process with the aim of classifying the existing building areas as green spaces. Notably for the first time the owner of the land on which the high-rise building now towers above the Wall signals his willingness to give up his land on the Spree and allow it to be used by the public if he is offered a comparable replacement plot. Once again assistance must be sought at government level because the district Council has neither the appropriate exchange plots nor millions of Euros for possible compensation. At the end of October 2012 there is a positive signal from the Senate Department for Urban Development, still headed by Senator Ingeborg Junge-Reyer. As the competent authority it raises no objections to the change of the development plan and the associated conversion into a green space. The owner of the high-rise property at the time had agreed to an exchange of plots. He awaits an offer from the Berlin Senate. The consortium which owns the 120 metre block is also prepared to exchange plots based on Franz Schulz's statement that he had the Berlin Senate behind him. On 30 October 2012 the decision to amend the development plan is made. But the dream of actually being able to prevent the development at the East Side Gallery lasts barely a month.

On 23 November 2012 Post arrives from the Finance Senator, Ulrich Nussbaum stating that the Berlin Senate won't be providing any finance or exchange properties. The Government administration "has not established" that the piece of land and the East Side Gallery are of significance for the city as a whole. An exchange of land is not supported by the Finance Senator. The district Council should buy the property if it wants to have a green space there. For this however there will be no financial support from regional Government. Further the option of a land exchange cannot be undertaken by the local Council alone as the most desirable real estate is part of the State assets. The district does not have enough money to buy land or pay compensation and Senator Nussbaum is well aware of this.

2013 Resistance

The owner of the site on which, according to building regulations the tower could be built immediately, sells to Maik Uwe Hinkel's CIC Group when it becomes clear that the Senate is not prepared to provide an exchange plot. But there was still one tiny glimmer of hope. After various extensions, the building permit for the tower would have expired in June 2013. Since the planning deadline according to BauGB expired after 7 years, this would have meant no legal entitlement to a further extension. It would certainly not have been extended again by the Council. Well obviously Mr. Hinkel also knew that and because it is sufficient in principle to drive a bulldozer over the construction site or dig around a little thus marking the start of construction, he did not hesitate for long. Behind the scenes, he obtained the necessary permission for a break in the Wall for vehicle access to the construction site which he could not be denied under existing building legislation. I don't remember the exact date, but I think it was one of the last days in February or at the beginning of March when I got a call in the morning: "Come quickly, they have started to tear down the Wall." It was quite a spooky atmosphere. There were surprisingly many people, almost all silent and kept at a distance by at least as many police officers and security forces. But there were more and more protesters and the work was interrupted at some point. Obviously nobody had expected so much resistance. This culminated in a major demonstration on March 17th 2013 which Roger Waters of Pink Floyd along with

6,000 people took part in. This resulted in the situation attracting a lot of attention not only in Berlin but also in the international press and among the general public.

We local Councillors together with the protesting civil population also tried to build up pressure on the Senate once again. First with a resolution addressed to the Senate which made it clear that the democratically elected representatives of the local Council also reject development:

"The local assembly of Friedrichshain-Kreuzberg as well as the Council has long been committed to ensuring that the former death strip behind the East Side Gallery is not built on. We want neither a skyscraper nor a 120-meter-long block. This development on the narrow green strip between the East Side Gallery and the banks of the Spree would make the historic Hinterland Wall with the East Side Gallery resemble a front garden wall in the presence of these concrete piles. This type of development also contravenes the successful peoples' referendum of 2008 and would separate the two parks on the banks of the Spree that have been created in recent years. This is why we decided last autumn to create a continuous public green space instead of a built-up area. This is the only way we can guarantee the preservation of the East Side Gallery. It was obvious to us last year that we didn't have the power at local Council level to change the plans and create a green space. We can only search for a replacement site for the current landowner in conjunction with the Senate. The banks of the River Spree are the heart of the city. It is not only a tourist magnet but also a place of recreation for Berliners and that is why we should work together to find a solution that is

beneficial to the citizens of Berlin. We therefore call on the Senate to seize this last chance and work together with the district of Friedrichshain-Kreuzberg for the East Side Gallery and against building development: A complete preservation of the East Side Gallery is only possible without buildings on the former death strip. The East Side Gallery must not become a garden wall for multi-storey buildings".

Furthermore, in the same session of the district council on March 20th 2013 an emergency motion was tabled and passed by a majority in which the local Council was once again called upon to sound out all possibilities and to make every effort to halt and permanently prevent the construction. This desperate attempt was again justified by the fact that:

"The protests of recent weeks and the petition against construction on the former death strip behind the East Side Gallery show that the local parliament of-Friedrichshain-Kreuzberg should make a further attempt to change the building legislation introduced by the Senate in 2001. The last attempt in autumn 2012 was destined to fail due to the lack of support from the Berlin Senate. The development can still be prevented if all political forces pull together on this issue. The district Council has neither the economic power nor the necessary exchange plots. Should the Senate fail to support the project, the local parliament, after scrutiny of the most accurate data at its disposal, will have to determine whether it can take responsibility for the Council going it alone under the present conditions and the threat of financial costs and possible legal consequences.

The East Side Gallery is threatened with deteriorating, from a world-famous memorial to the division of Berlin and the joy of overcoming it to the front garden wall of a massive building over 120 metres long, towering over it. More than 75,000 have signed a petition and spoken out against this development, more than 6,000 people took to the streets on 3rd March 2013 and again on 17th March in the successful peoples' referendum "Spreeufer für alle" (Banks of the Spree for all) in 2008 when 87% voted against the development .

There can be no doubt that:

1. *The great majority of the local population who voted in 2008 rejected this development and wanted an undeveloped riverbank behind the Wall.*
2. *The Senate administration's assessment that this is not a project of interest to the city as a whole is false.*
3. *This isn't just about an area of interest for the city as a whole but as the reports and activities in social media in recent weeks have shown, a unique monument of international interest. It must not only be protected from further breaches but also from disappearing into a general collective, an indistinct mass, that will forever damage the distinctiveness of this special place."*

A matter for the boss: Klaus Wowereit's hour

Due to public pressure and the intervention of the rebellious district Council, Klaus Wowereit, the Governing Mayor of Berlin declares without further ado that the preservation of the East Side Gallery is a matter for the boss. The result is deplorable: the property owners of the planned 120-metre building complex are allowed to add another two floors to the building but instead of two openings in the Wall there will only be one which can be used as access by both parties. The Governing Mayor and Cultural Senator in a personal alliance had obviously still not understood - or simply did not want to - that this wasn't just about the breaks in the Wall but about the actual building projects. But the Governing Mayor of Berlin and his Building Senator Michael Müller, (today's head of government), continue to give this their unwavering support. The objection to the project from the Local Monument Protection Authority was dismissed by the State Monument Office. On the morning of 27th March 2013 four further segments were removed under police protection, creating a six-metre-wide access road to the construction site. In the following months, the local parliament and the protesters could only look on helplessly as the luxury white residential tower block grew floor by floor above the East Side Gallery - but not entirely.

2013 The West Side Gallery

With a further local parliament resolution we immediately made it clear that the district Council was not going to take any administrative action which would support Klaus Wowereit's "deal" which would ultimately only lead to an increase in the building size. We also took a constructive approach with the West Side Gallery project to show what kind of space would be destroyed here over and above the historical heritage of the Wall and the East Side Gallery. Together with curator Adrienne Goehler we tried for over two years to turn the bare rear side of the East Side Gallery into a place of artistic exploration with themes such as the Wall, the Fall of the Wall, division, borders, and migration; themes which in our opinion, could, when dealing with the issue of present-day borders, achieve a particular impact and publicity through their placement on the former Wall. Our efforts had failed up to that point because of the protection of historical monument status and the fear that the monument would be damaged. This of course has now been made totally absurd with yet another break in the Wall. Thus on 10th July 2013 Kai Wiedenhöfer's exhibition 'Wall on Wall' photographs of existing and proposed borders was printed on paper and attached to the rear of the Wall whilst next to us a luxury residential project was taking shape. From June to September 2016, another project by Kai Wiedenhöfer and Adrienne Goehler was exhibited there: 'War on Wall' a response to the increasingly defensive reactions to the so-called "refugee crisis," disturbing images of the destruction of Kobane and of injured people from the war in Syria were shown.

Thus for a second time the rear of the East Side Gallery became a backdrop for an artistic appeal for more humanity and empathy with current refugees in a place that was once historically meant to prevent people from fleeing. In retrospect, it seems somehow fitting that this exhibition took place just at the time of the district and House of Representatives elections in 2016, which led to a government alliance of SPD, the Left and Alliance 90/The Greens.

2016 Apparent rethink

For the first time through the coalition of SPD, the Left and Alliance 90/The Greens, there was a clear commitment to the East Side Gallery on the part of the State. Perhaps not least because with Antje Kapek as co-faction leader, Daniel Wesener as parliamentary group leader and cultural-political spokesman, and six other Friedrichshain-Kreuzberg MPs, there were now people involved in the coalition agreement negotiations who had all been active in local politics at one time or another and who had already campaigned for the East Side Gallery. As a result the coalition agreement of the new government alliance concluded:

"The coalition is committed to the continuous preservation of the remains of the Wall and the green space at the East Side Gallery as well as to negotiations with the investors regarding exchange plots of land. The works of art are to be maintained, regularly restored and in addition the information onsite will be expanded upon"

After we, ie. in particular we Greens, had been campaigning in vain for years both in the district Council, in the local parliament and at the State level to obtain support and financial resources from the Berlin State for the preservation and maintenance of the East Side Gallery and to prevent further devaluation of the monument by the colossal buildings there, we suddenly appeared to have consensus. Unfortunately this turned out to be an illusion because the Senate administration responsible for the implementation of these promises - Finance, Urban Development, Culture and Monument Protection -

remained in the hands of the SPD and the Left who then subsequently let us fail.

Spring 2017 The district Council takes the initiative

To ensure that the promises made in the coalition agreement didn't just remain a nice but non-binding declaration of intent, we of course took action immediately after the agreement came into force. After all, the responsibility for the East Side Gallery and the prevailing building regulations still lay, at least nominally, with the local Council. Thus in spring 2017 we submitted three applications to the local parliament. In addition to the applications to propose the ESG for inclusion in the UNESCO World Cultural Heritage and to initiate the development of a comprehensive concept for the East Side Gallery, of particular importance was the application to secure the undeveloped land at the East Side Gallery. In this respect the local Council in consultation with the relevant Senate administration is instructed to immediately take steps to "safeguard and preserve the remains of the Wall and the green space at the East Side Gallery." In July 2017 the application was approved by the local parliament and forwarded to the responsible senate administrations for finance, culture and monument protection as well as urban development.

Then once again nothing happened which is why during the meeting of the district council in September I asked the question "what steps have been taken so far to implement the decision of 12.7.2017 to secure the still undeveloped areas at the East Side Gallery." The question about the state of play was explicit and answered by our city Councillor for construction, Florian Schmidt:

"In a letter dated 30.8.2017 I suggested several steps for implementing the objectives contained in the Senate's and District Council's coalition agreement to Senators Dr. Kollatz-Ahnen, Lederer and Lompscher.

"Steps 2-4 would probably have to be carried out in tandem.

1. Agreement between Senate and district Council, as to how the provisions set out in the coalition agreement can be complied with and the planned new hotel building and further development of the former "death strip" prevented.

2. Examination of the legal possibilities to prevent the construction of the hotel, including the determination of the level of compensation.

3. Identification of exchange plots.

4. Opening negotiations with new owners.

A response to the letter is pending. If there is no agreement between the Senate and the district Council, the Council cannot take any further steps. Building projects where the building permits have already been granted can only be stopped if appropriate compensatory amounts or equivalent plots of land are made available by the Senate."

This was not the only reason why in September 2017 we made specific amendments and submitted an application to become active as a district to revive the procedure for altering the development plan which had lain dormant since its preliminary approval in 2013. Meanwhile, the new investor, Trockland Management Ltd announced at the beginning of August 2018 that it would begin construction of the development project

"Pier 61/63," the 120-metre block. They had obviously noticed that things could get tight.

Autumn 2017 and yet everything is just as it was

Lo and behold in October there was a reaction from the Senate, namely a written response from Senator Katrin Lompscher herself in which it was admitted that in principle it was possible to designate areas at the ESG as green spaces by amending the development plan but that this would be quite expensive, namely 60 million Euros. It should be mentioned, that according to the Construction Senator, only about half of the 60 million would have been due as direct compensation for the withdrawal of the building permit, the planning costs incurred to date and the purchase of the site by the State. The vast remainder would have been for possible civil damages "for lost corporate profit" for the "economic operational phase of the hotel and the apartments". But even if it was initially only a matter of the potential, hypothetical and probable due costs to the State the application was then rejected and finally sunk in the decisive local parliament session on 13.12.2017. And that with only one majority vote. It was expected that the front of SPD, FDP, CDU and AfD would oppose our proposal as was the certain fact that we Greens would support the resolution recommending the reopening of the development plan process. In the end the decisive factor was the conduct of the left-wing faction. Here, three group members took a stand against our motion, two were in favour and a further two abstained. So the result was 20:19. This meant that the Senate Departments for Finance and Urban Development could wash their hands of the responsibility and shift the blame onto the local Council, according to the maxim: look, not even the local Council is in favour of preventing further development at the East Side Gallery at this price.

Officially, this decision was justified in particular by the delegates of the SPD and the Left, who had voted against the reopening of the development plan process, on the grounds that the 60 million which could be due in compensation brought into play by Mrs. Lompscher was simply too much. Further they argued that these millions could be used more sensibly or would be unavailable for more important things such as schools and day-care centres. This is of course complete nonsense in view of the budget surpluses currently generated. But once again it makes very clear the significance attached to the East Side Gallery, in no way that of an important and unique monument to and triumph over partition which must be preserved in its impact for future generations. Quite apart from the fact that the Trockland Investors would appear to have excellent connections at their disposal when one realises that here in Berlin, with Checkpoint Charlie, they are allowed to destroy yet another monument for their commercial interests without the State intervening.

A political misjudgement?

Perhaps the desire to instruct the district Council to act on a further specific local parliament decision, namely the reopening of the development plan process to reclassify the development site as a green area, was simply a mistake. After all, in principle there already was such a resolution to which the district Council could have referred and also an answer from the responsible senate administrations that this was possible and permissible in principle, as well as a precise estimate of the compensation costs. But there was just no explicit statement as to how the Senate administrations for Finance or Urban development would react, should the district take the initiative. The district Council would have needed such an undertaking to pay compensation or provide a substitute site neither of which it had at its disposal and it quite obviously shied away from the risk of incurring costs at a later date that could not have been covered from the district budget without the agreement of the Senate. In short, I feared simply that once again nothing would happen, that letters would go back and forth while Trockland was busy creating a fait accompli on the basis of the current, still valid building permit. I believe at that moment when the local parliament officially decided to reopen the development plan process, the district Council could have imposed a ban on changes, which would have prevented this. I just didn't want to get another phone call like the one in spring 2013 and have to stand stunned and powerless at the East Side Gallery and have to watch it all start again.

And so in order to force the district Council to take the first step and then also force *r2g in the Senate and House of Representatives to adopt a clear position on the assumption that they would not act against the promises made in their coalition agreement I introduced this proposal. I simply hadn't reckoned that colleagues in my own constituency from the SPD and the Left would put a spoke in the wheel and thus relieve their own people in the Senate of the responsibility. And I still can't fathom it.

Werner Heck

Perhaps a government propped up by the Left and the Greens despite an already dwindling SPD would have reacted differently to massive protests from civil society. But apart from a very active and committed "Monument to Joy" initiative that had its roots in *Mediaspree Versenken*, a few artists and a few activists from the civil rights movement of the former GDR, it seemed that hardly anyone was interested in what was happening to the East Side Gallery. It was actually odd at a time of widespread resistance against the sellout of the city. But perhaps in the case of the East Side Gallery "the deed had already been done," as the chairman of the Friedrichshain-Kreuzberger city planning committee put it on the occasion of the vote to reopen the development plan process. And most of the activists have long since abandoned the East Side Gallery, perhaps because they don't think it is worth spending millions on since - apart from the paintings, which are no longer originals - there's hardly anything left of what once made this place so special.

But perhaps things will change when construction work on the project Pier 61/63 really gets going and people see what it does to this unique monument. The nine-storey, one hundred and twenty metre long block will not only encroach on the East Side Gallery but also tower above it. I'm just afraid it will then be too late. But I don't like to just give up either.

Werner Heck

*r2g – the red/red/green political coalition formed from SPD/ Left&Alliance 90/ the Greens

The bridge

The Oberbaum bridge is one of the most, if not the most, beautiful bridges in Berlin. It unites the districts of Friedrichshain and Kreuzberg as it spans the River Spree. The bridge is at the beginning of the East Side Gallery and during the reign of the Wall had been used as a pedestrian border crossing which took you to the district of Kreuzberg (36) on the west side. This border crossing wasn't however for use by tourists. It was used for the exchange of political prisoners and also enabled GDR citizens of pensionable age to cross to the West.

In autumn 1964 (three years after the Berlin Wall was erected), the GDR Government decided to allow Pensioners to travel to West Berlin or West Germany for a maximum of four weeks a year to visit relatives. The ruling applied to women aged 60 and above and for men aged 65 and above. You couldn't just turn up at a border crossing but had of course to apply for a visitors permit in advance. It didn't take long for several thousand Pensioners to take advantage of this new arrangement.

This new ruling sadly excluded anyone who didn't have any relatives in the West. It was some twenty years later, in 1984 that Pensioners could apply for a permit for the purpose of visiting friends. You wonder if after over twenty years of division anyone in the East had any friends left in the West?

Pensioners who took advantage of the chance to visit the West could of course have chosen not to return. It was however the uncertainty and fear of what reprisals the GDR authorities would take against family left behind in the East that brought people back. Fear was the mechanism which allowed the few to control the many.

The bridge

If you were successful in moving to the West permanently then you would receive your pension from the West German Government. The East German authorities were probably glad to get rid of you as you would have been considered more of a burden than an asset and your permanent move to the West meant they no longer had to pay you a Pension. If you left a home behind then that was an even bigger bonus for them as housing was scarce in the East. If you did decide to remain in the West then you could simply hand in your GDR passport and register with one of the reception centres set up for that purpose. If you had relatives or friends in the West then the procedure went quite quickly because according to the law of the FRG (Federal Republic of Germany) the citizens of the GDR were already (West) German citizens.

After German reunification on 3rd October 1990 the Pension Law was quietly amended. Up to that point the Pensions for political refugees from the GDR had been the same as those for citizens of the FRG. Under this amendment the former citizens of the GDR had to put up with a loss of between 150 and 600 DM per month. Nice "brotherly" act!

When we started work on the Gallery, the Oberbaum bridge was impassable, being completely sealed off at both ends, unlike now where the bridge conveys what seems a constant flow of motorised traffic and the U-bahn (overground at this point) from one side of the river to the other. We also had no access to the rear of the Wall and thus to the riverside. The actual crossing used by Pensioners was a narrow, covered walkway over part of the bridge. The guard house and crossing were still in use when we started painting East Side Gallery and

The bridge

we eventually persuaded the guards to store our ladder and pots of paint and to allow us to use their toilet until the border unit was closed completely.

Waiting for someone? The border exit point on the west side of the Oberbaum bridge.

Photo credits:Robert-Havemann-Gesellschaft/
Bernd Markowsky RHG_Fo_BEMA_1272a

Supermarkets ransacked

In the days and weeks following the opening of the Wall, the supermarkets in the West part of Berlin looked as though they had been ransacked. Instead of neatly stocked, full shelves there were rows and rows of empty shelves. The people in the West had never seen anything like it. The East Berliners had literally stripped the shelves of anything they could get their hands on.

Living in the communist controlled east part of Berlin meant that very little was imported (because of lack of hard currency) and when it came to food, fresh fruit and vegetables were a rare commodity. Some of the fruit and vegetables I had seen on sale there (during the four years I had worked in East Berlin) would have been thrown in the bin and certainly not displayed in any shop in the west of the city. But what do you do if that is all that you can get?

Whenever you saw a queue in the East you immediately joined it not knowing what it was for. Queues usually meant that something was on sale which was rarely available. So, whatever it was, you could be fairly sure you wanted some of it. Everyone carried a little cloth shopping bag at all times as there was no such thing as plastic carrier bags. If anything required to be wrapped then it was grey paper tied with string or paper bags which was used. The Shopper might also have brought paper or paper bags with them which were then reused.

It was during my time working at the Embassy that I became aware of the buying power which we have in the West because

Supermarkets ransacked

there was no such thing in the East. You could walk into shops where there were literally a handful of items on the shelves. You had no choice. You took what you could get when it was available. In the West we do have choice. Our buying power is one of the few powers which we have in a capitalist society yet few people use that power with discernment and many seem totally unaware that they have it.

Disillusion

Not everything was rosy in this country which was slowly knitting itself back together. The coming together of two related but dissimilar folk didn't find favour with everyone. Many West Berliners were becoming increasingly annoyed at finding their supermarket shelves empty and being stuck in permanent traffic jams. Congestion was the operative word in the West. The undergrounds were always packed, traffic was in a constant jam and queuing was unavoidable. Queuing in the East had been an integral part of everyday life; in the West it was an unwelcome change. Tempers were raised, nerves frayed at the edges.

The initial euphoric welcome extended to the brothers and sisters from the East was sadly waning. The West Berliner's daily routine was greatly disrupted. A certain amount of resentment against the East Germans started to build. I remember being surprised at this and questioned how I would feel if my country, Scotland had been divided for years and then reunited. Would I not be overjoyed for everyone? A complete change in routine is very difficult for some to deal with it seems, even when the change is so momentous and positive. Change can't always be controlled or organised of course. As we were literally working on the street, the Artists and I picked up on the growing feelings of disenchantment among the East German citizens.

Unsettling stories were going round about East Germans leaving their husbands, wives and even children behind in the East and disappearing to the West. It appeared outwardly that when the communists were in power the East Germans had a strong social cohesion but when these things started to happen

Disillusion

it seemed to raise doubts that it was a genuine social conscience that they had. Was it more a case of when you are in the same boat then you behave accordingly? It certainly hadn't been an egalitarian society, for those at the top (eg Party Members) had enjoyed privileges the ordinary citizens could only fantasise about.

Elections

In March 1990 the weather became kinder. It was easier to paint when you could feel your fingers. The first democratic elections took place in the East. This added to our bureaucratic nightmare, as in common with many other countries during election fervour, nobody wanted to make a decision or take responsibility for anything, everything was in limbo. This meant that we couldn't get anyone to decide on the fate of the Gallery.

The elections also brought an unwanted practical issue for us. As with most election campaigns posters were being put up everywhere promoting various candidates and political parties. As you can imagine the Wall was a very inviting backdrop for these posters so rows of them covered the East Side Gallery, like wallpaper. They had been glued on and removing them, which we had to do to prepare the surface for the artists, was a filthy, sticky, messy job which I experienced firsthand having helped some of the artists do it. The cold weather didn't improve the task any. Somehow freezing cold goo is more disgusting than warm goo

I hear what you are feeling

Working at the East Side Gallery meant that we were literally working on the street. The Oberbaum bridge situated at the beginning of the Gallery was still used as a border crossing for East Germans for some months after the Wall opened. Every day queues of East Berliners formed on the pavement next to the artists whilst waiting to cross the bridge on foot this being quicker than driving. The artists who were sometimes there for hours working on their paintings couldn't help but overhear the conversations of the waiting throng. This definitely influenced some of the artists in their work, as they were witnessing the changing emotions, opinions and beliefs that many East German citizens had held about the West. Disenchantment was setting in. It was no longer seen by some as a Paradise with gold-plated pavements. The East and its citizens "Easties" (Ossies) also found themselves being treated as second class by some of those from the West - "Westies" (Wessies).

After the Wall opened the West more or less took the East over, just gobbled it up. It wasn't a coming together of equals, far from it. There was such arrogance about the attitude of many in the West towards anything connected with the East in general. In their eyes, everything and everyone from the East was inferior. I don't think many people in the West were aware then or even now that many goods for sale in the West were actually manufactured in the East. Tobacco was shipped in from Cuba and processed in the East before being enclosed in familiar western packaging and transported to the West. western brands of schnapps underwent a similar process and a well known furniture company gave prisoners in the East the pleasure of constructing their flatpacks.

There was however one East German thing that the West failed to remove – despite attempting to – the wee green and red man on the pedestrian crossing lights! The Ampelmann as he is called was such a distinctive iconic thing really. He is nothing like those you see in the West. When the pedestrian light is red his arms are stretched out to the side in a "blocking" gesture and when it is green he is seen walking. Certainly quite clear to anyone who may perhaps be colour blind.

Diary entry 7.5.90

Sometimes I wonder if I am doing the right thing with the Gallery. I get so tired and feel so alone and then something happens which makes me think it has to be

Diary entry 16.5.90

Feel much better today. Had a good sleep. Went over to Checkpoint Charlie for the first time in ages as I had to take Kikue over the border. We spent about 45 minutes in the rain at ESG while Kikue was interviewed by Japanese TV. Note: I had been using another border crossing nearer ESG which is why I hadn't been over Checkpoint Charlie for a while.

Permission to come over

In May I still had to notify the Border Control (Grenz-kommando) when I was taking foreign painters to the East. Details of their Nationalities and passports had to be supplied in advance and the intended border crossing specified. I think there is a tendency to think that the borders opened wide on November 9th all the guards left and that was it. That isn't what happened. There was a gradual loosening of, rather than an immediate relinquishing of control. A temporary border was still in place until July 1st 1990 so people still had to show ID in order to cross before the borders disappeared completely and controls ceased to exist. It may have been a mere formality but it was there nonetheless. The border at Checkpoint Charlie was removed on June 22nd 1990 with lots of pomp and circus as you can perhaps imagine. It was after all in the American sector.

Diary entry 29.5.90

Catrin Resch arrives in the evening. She is staying with me while she does her painting. For the first time I had a feeling of oneness, of calmness while at ESG. When collecting Catrin it was about 9pm and the traffic had died down a bit, obviously contributing to the calmness but that wasn't the whole reason. There wasn't the usual feeling of loneliness of being completely on my own with this Wall. Somehow the pictures and I seemed one – difficult to explain.

All change

Can you imagine everything in your life changing as drastically as it did for the East Germans overnight? One minute you can't cross to the West at all and the next the borders are open, like prison gates being cast aside. Everything seemed to change so fast in that first year after the Fall of the Wall. I remember driving round corners and thinking, "Where did that building go?" or, "Where did that new one come from?" Berlin seemed like a constantly changing canvas.

There were few roads joining East and West Berlin at that time so the volume of traffic was horrendous and you could get stuck in traffic jams for ages. It was often quicker to walk over to the other side and use public transport. The public transport systems in East and West were, for obvious reasons, completely separate. Before East and West Berlin were divided by the Wall some of the train lines were connected but that had all changed after the Wall went up.

In the 28 years that the Wall was all-encompassing, there were some underground lines that began their journey in the West and went through the East without stopping. These lines went from the West through the East and then back to the West. If you pressed your face against the window whilst travelling on these lines and peered into the darkness, you could just make out the armed soldiers standing on the dark, dusty, abandoned platforms in the East as you flashed by. What a deadly boring job standing in a cold, dark, empty station for hours just in case someone tried to use the tunnel to escape to the West. The East Germans were not aware that these lines ran under them; the entrances above ground were bricked up.

All change

Berlin was already a divided city before the Wall went up. It had been so since after the Second World War when the "Winners" the Russians, French, British and Americans carved the city up into "their" respective sectors. The West was jointly under the control of the French, British and Americans who had their allocated zones within it and the East was the Russian controlled sector. A border control mechanism was in place before the Wall went up so you couldn't just hop across from West to East or vice versa without identity documents. As there was a huge exodus of people from the Russian controlled sector in East Berlin and from the whole of East Germany which was also under Russian military control to the West where living conditions were better, the Wall was put up to quite literally cement an already existing division.

The Public transport system then was also separated into East and West so you would take a bus to the checkpoint from either side where you would have to get off, show your papers, go through the control and then get into a bus on the other side. You could however use the S-Bahn to get from one sector to the other as it ran in both East and West.

The division of Berlin cut streets in half both lengthwise and widthwise. Some houses on the border were cleared, rivers, people, places all found themselves in a different country without having moved physically. Dividing an already existing city isn't an orderly boxing up. That would be impossible. You don't end up with neat straight lines everywhere, more snake-like zigzags which follow district boundaries. The east/west divide wasn't geographical as East Berlin was in the North and West Berlin in the south.

All change

Before monetary union on July 1ˢᵗ 1990 when the East Mark ceased to have any value and the Deutschmark was the currency of unity, the citizens from the East flocked to the West to go shopping where they could buy, for them, previously unseen treasures. Some East Germans also found work in the West and sometimes became cheap labour for many businesses there. Border crossers would park their cars on the wide pavement in front of the Gallery and walk across the bridge to catch a bus or travel by U-Bahn or S-Bahn. This was often quicker in the early days after the Wall opened than driving across one of the former checkpoints.

The only joined up roads between East and West Berlin had been checkpoints and there were few of them. (It wasn't as if the authorities could suddenly conjure up new roads.) More roads became available as the Wall was removed. The parked cars on the pavement in front of the Gallery seriously hampered the artists' work. It was difficult for them to paint in the narrow space between the parked car and the Wall and they couldn't properly view their work from a distance. When they crossed to the other side of the wide road to get another perspective, half of their painting was obscured by a parked car. To overcome this difficulty I often went to the Wall around midnight the night before artists were planning to work or when the photographer was scheduled to take photos knowing there would be no parked cars there at that time. I then tied a rope between some of the streetlights to prevent cars parking on the pavement. This was one of the rare occasions when the road was fairly quiet and one of my favourite times there. There was a tremendous feeling of oneness. The energy and message of each individual painting came across strongly, undisturbed by traffic noise and pollution. It took nine months to complete the painting of the East Side Gallery and in that time it completely took over my life, getting right under my skin. Somewhere along the way I was given the name "The Mother of the Gallery."

Cesar Olhagaray (with gasmask) and Jens-Helge Dahmen at work with queuing East Germans waiting to cross the border.

Relationship to money

In the East basic foodstuffs like bread, milk, margarine and some types of fish such as herring and carp had been subsidised. A shortage of money wasn't usually the big issue; it was lack of something to spend it on. The GDR didn't have a lot of hard currency so what they had wasn't spent on anything they considered unnecessary or a luxury.

The average time you had to wait for a car was around ten years if you lived in Berlin and twelve years if you didn't. It was best to pass your driving test at age eighteen and then immediately order a car. You could usually get the Trabant model quicker and that was also the most affordable model at around 10,000-12,000 East Marks. Non foodstuffs were made to last and people really looked after things because if something broke or was damaged there was no guarantee you would find a replacement for it.

It was because lack of money wasn't really an issue for them that many East Germans falsely assumed that we in the West had unlimited supplies of money and that we could afford to buy anything we wanted. I remember when I worked in the British Embassy how an East German colleague asked me to buy things for her with no regard for the cost.

It was only when East Germans came over to the West and especially after they got their "welcome money" (Begrüssungs-geld - each East German citizen received 100 Deutschmarks when they moved to the West permanently, something which existed for Pensioners even before the Wall opened but was now given to all) that disillusionment crept in. When they received their welcome money they probably thought, "Wow 100 DM I am rich and I can buy anything!" All those things which hadn't been available to them seemed now to be within reach. For some East Germans, visiting the West for the first time, with all its razzle dazzle and sparkle, was just too much for them. They broke down in tears at the sight of all the shops overflowing with goods and eating places offering a seemingly unlimited variety and amount of foods many of which they had never seen before. The gulf between the East and West in that respect just couldn't have been further apart.

The actual coins which were GDR currency were made of very cheap light metal, obviously cheap to produce. The banknotes were really small. It looked and felt like pretend money from a board game. You couldn't really envisage it being the legal currency of an actual country if you were used to large banknotes and coins which were a lot heavier and made of more expensive metals. I doubt if anyone ever tried to forge it.

But there were other scams and illegal ways to increase your wealth. The official exchange rate during the Wall's existence was 1 Mark (East) to 1 DM (West) and with Monetary Union on July 1st 1990 East German citizens were allowed to exchange savings of up to 6,000 Marks into DM at a rate of 1:1 with amounts above that exchanged at 2 Marks for 1 DM. This was exploited by people from both East and West. A substantial profit was made by getting around 4 Marks for 1 DM on the black market and then changing the Marks back to DM at the official exchange rate of 1:1. Every East German citizen who had savings of less than 6,000 Marks was eagerly sought after by citizens from East and West to have their accounts topped up to a maximum of 6,000 DM with both sharing the spoils.

.

Wall-StreetGallery

Claudia Croon, current co-creator of Wall-StreetGallery and Peter Unsicker

Peter Unsicker is the very gifted sculptor and artist who owns Wall-StreetGallery in Zimmerstrasse where he has lived and worked for over thirty years. He opened the Gallery on November 9th 1986 exactly three years to the day before the Berlin Wall surrendered its function. Peter felt he had to do something about the grey mass of Wall which greeted him every morning so he consulted the I Ching (Chinese book of Changes) for guidance as to what action he should take. The answer he received to his request was the I Ching symbol no 18 Ku *Work on what has been Spoiled*. So for several years Peter created and attached installations to the Wall which was about 1.5 metres in front of his gallery in Zimmerstrasse (just yards from Checkpoint Charlie).

His first work was a mask of a child's face with a sticking plaster beside it as though the face was emerging from the Wall wounded. This was promptly removed by the East German guards. Peter responded by putting two masks on the Wall and then when they were removed he again doubled the number of masks. The Allies, particularly the Americans and the British also "stole" some of his masks, probably as souvenirs. Peter had various installations on his section of Wall over the years and with these he probably succeeded in annoying the East German authorities. In the end they gave up and stopped removing his artwork.

It was forbidden to paint damage or attach anything to the Wall but the East Germans couldn't do anything to Peter because he lived in the West although technically he could have been arrested in front of his Gallery. There was a sign at Checkpoint Charlie which said "Enter Zimmerstrasse at your own risk." If the East German authorities had wanted to arrest him then they could easily have done that in East Berlin as he was a frequent visitor there. It would have been easier for the Americans to arrest him without reason. That was allied law in Berlin. This allied law also permitted the allies to shoot anyone who didn't have an identity card.

After the borders opened one of Peter's exhibitions was of photographs documenting the East German guards and others removing the artwork he had attached to the Wall.

Wall-StreetGallery

Photo: Peter Unsicker – Masks on the Wall

It's commonly thought that the Wall marked the actual border between East and West but that wasn't the case. There was an area on the west side of the Wall which was east terrain. This varied in size but it meant that the East Germans could patrol along the west-facing side of the Wall to check on their "property."

The "street" (Zimmerstrasse), which was just a wide pavement, was a bit like a corridor with the Wall on one side and flats, mostly with shop fronts at street level on the other. The Gallery was long and narrow and Peter's living area was at the back of the gallery and the gallery was always open.

Wall-StreetGallery

The front of Peter's Gallery which consisted wholly of glass, a window and a glass door was the actual border so that when he stepped out of his front door he was in the East but he had a back door which was in the West. At that time he could go out the back door and walk through wasteland to get onto Kochstrasse. Now his only entry and exit point is the front door because the area at the back has been filled with modern flats. The East Germans couldn't come to his back door and the West German police and officials couldn't come to his front door. The Allies could knock on both.

Peter held a party when the Wall sections in front of his gallery were removed. He *"Boxed the Wall up"* in wood as though ready for despatch. It was when they removed the Wall there that I realised how thin it actually had been. I had always imagined (probably like many others) that it was about 3 feet thick everywhere when actually in many places it was nearer 6 inches (about 15cm). It was a bit like an optical illusion. On top of the Wall there was a rounded section, a bit like half a huge pipe and at the bottom, on the east side, there were concrete "feet" about 1m long which would have made it impossible for someone to topple the Wall by driving into it. So when you looked at it face on it gave the illusion of being very thick from top to bottom – insurmountable.

Zimmerstrasse, like so many streets in Berlin has now been well and truly yuppified with much of its character and individuality destroyed. Wall-StreetGallery in contrast, is like a wonderful oasis for the eye, the mind and soul, like a light shining in the darkness....

The Wall in front of Wall-StreetGallery being dismantled

The Wall must go – or maybe not

At some point in summer 1990 there was an official announcement that the Wall at Mühlenstrasse was going to be removed. The *Magistrat* informed wuva that it was to be dismantled by 31st December 1990. Everything changed so quickly in the first year after the Wall fell. There was no precedent to follow so decisions on many issues were being made and then changed again shortly after. So there we were halfway through the creation of the Gallery and someone in "Authority" had decided it had to go.

The idea was then hatched that we dismantle the Gallery after its completion and send it on a world tour. This might sound a bit crazy but we did some research got some quotes and found out that it was not as impractical as it sounded. It was hoped that the Gallery would return to Berlin after the tour and be offered a permanent location by the Senate but if that wasn't going to happen then the paintings were to be auctioned on tour completion with 50% of the profits from the project to be given to cultural institutions and a school for the deaf in Friedrichshain.

Of course that idea was shelved when the Authorities changed their mind and the Gallery was allowed to remain where it was. The decision for the World Tour was made as a solution, a way to save the East Side Gallery from complete destruction by the Authorities, as that had appeared to be their official plan at that time. You could argue that the Berlin Authorities never gave up their plan to destroy the East Side Gallery and just did it a bit at a time .

Remembering where it was

In the early months after 9th November 1989 the call for the removal of all traces of the Wall was almost unanimous. The slogan "the Wall must go" seemed to become fashionable in the media. Some sections of the Wall in the centre were then whipped away really quickly. However, this resulted in visitors asking where it previously stood so that cobblestones and plaques were eventually put into the ground in some places, marking the spot. A few segments of Wall were even brought back to Checkpoint Charlie.

There were however, even at that point, a few voices who argued for some of the Wall to be retained as a memorial so that future generations knew what it looked like and what had happened there. Sections of the Wall which were retained for this purpose form part of the Memorial at Bernauer Strasse.

It's strange how quickly you forget where something was, even something as massive as a Wall over 3m high but it happens. It is very fortunate therefore that sections of the Wall were retained.

I remember walking along Zimmerstrasse, near Checkpoint Charlie one day, not long after the Wall came down. A tourist approached me and asked me where the Wall had been. I had to admit that I couldn't answer immediately until I noticed the "scars" in the tarmac where it once stood. This incident confirmed my belief in the importance of retaining a sufficiently long stretch of the Berlin Wall so that its size, appearance and impact can be appreciated by those who weren't alive then. It is very difficult to envisage otherwise what it was like to live on either side of it and to imagine how that affected peoples' lives.

Remembering where it was

The East Side Gallery is the longest remaining piece of the Berlin Wall (at least it was until the Berlin Authorities allowed sections to be removed).

Unlike the Wall pieces at Bernauer Strasse however, the East Side Gallery is not a reminder of the terror and death caused by the Wall and a repressive regime rather an object of hope as to how something can be transformed.

Diary entry 8.6.90

A very welcome day off. It rained constantly over the weekend, so heavy that the rain came in through my closed windows. It fitted my mood exactly and gave me a break – I obviously couldn't go to the Wall when it was raining. It made me feel like being back in Scotland. I felt a bit cocooned, could withdraw and be on my own again.

West influence

Peter Nagelschmidt/Christine MacLean/Rainer Uhlmann
Photo Mary Mackey.

Diary entry 21.6 90

*The border becomes more and more open day by day. They
don't even look at your papers any more. There is a big
symbolic happening at Checkpoint Charlie when they remove
the Allied huts.*

Diary entry 1.7.90

*So many changes in Berlin, no borders, traffic jams. Violence,
crime, demonstrations.*

West influence

In July Peter Nagelschmidt arrived from West Germany to be given the post of Project Manager. I don't know why he replaced Andreas Dademasch. I wasn't involved in any of the politics of that.

Diary entry Friday 13.7.1990

Very, very tired emotionally and mentally. So many things have been happening. Andreas Dademasch (East German) has been replaced by Peter Nagelschmidt (West German) as my partner at wuva. Yesterday was a big meeting of the people from Geithain (the Agricultural Co-operative Geithain were wuva's majority shareholder). It was so tiring just waiting.

Today Peter Nagelschmidt took over. He, Rainer and I discussed my contract and my supposed new wage. I don't know who to trust anymore, or who to believe. Monty phoned yesterday wanting the T-shirts he ordered but didn't pay for. I feel in the middle of all these people being torn from side to side.

Communication

In these days of mobile phones with the expectation that you need to be available 24 hours a day (what a nightmare), it is probably difficult to imagine what it was like not to be able to contact someone whenever you wanted. Trying to phone from the East to the West (and vice versa) was a lesson in patience. There were simply few telephone lines available. One reason was that the communists probably didn't want their citizens contacting anyone in the "wicked" West. The other was probably that having a limited number of lines meant they needed fewer people to eavesdrop so getting an open line could take hours. I had already experienced this firsthand when I worked at the British Embassy in East Berlin.

The World media was finding it impossible to contact us in the East so Rainer Uhlmann, the director of wuva decided that we needed an office in the West. Don't forget that emails were still like science fiction then, we only had a fax which also needed a phone line to function so we moved into an office on the Potsdamerstrasse in the west part of Berlin whilst the main wuva office remained in the East.

The premises at 81B Potsdamerstrasse had previously been used by the short-lived English language magazine *Berliner*. I had worked for this magazine for a few months and knew that the offices were no longer being used as the owner had run into financial difficulties and suspended production. The furniture and some equipment were still there so we didn't have to go out and purchase anything. It suited our temporary requirements perfectly.

Communication

There were several willing volunteers who helped at the East Side Gallery, from midsummer onwards. Mary Mackey, although one of the artists of ESG mucked in as did Adam, Maya, Mark and Dominic. Some of them were employed briefly, others were just happy to be around and volunteer for a short while. They all found a bed or at least somewhere to sleep at my place for varying lengths of time.

Diary entry 31.7
I'm very tired. I've even lost interest in ESG. I've had a cold for the last 5 days which doesn't help matters. Met Maja, Mark and Dominic who stayed here for a few days.

Things are changing so fast. Don't know what the future holds for me or ESG. Feel trapped at the moment – long to get away. Badly need a holiday.

Few, if any of the artists were paid for their work although a payment of 500 DM per artist was written into their contracts with wuva. Those coming from further afield had to pay all their own travel and accommodation costs. Some of the artists who didn't live in Berlin stayed with me whilst they painted their murals so that their financial outlay could be kept to a minimum.

After my friend and flatmate Rita moved to Amsterdam to be with her beloved I was left alone in a large flat. It meant that I had the space to offer several ESG artists and some unofficial helpers who arrived in summer somewhere to stay. Among these were Günther Schaefer, Catrin Resch, Kikue Miyatake, Adam, Dominic, Maya and Mark.

Slow build up to Wall opening

The most difficult adjustment for the new citizens of the West was probably the psychological one. Imagine living your entire life in a prison or being brainwashed to believe certain things which determined how you had lived your life up to that point and then one day realising that you were living in a false reality and that your entire life was based on a lie. How would you cope with that? Add to that the fact that the Stasi weren't punished or even held accountable for the way they had treated you and your fellow citizens and maybe ended up in the police force in the West or in the new Government. How would that make you feel? Considering that our identity is closely tied to our tribe/family, country and culture, what effect does it have on our identity when our country disappears? It must have been a great shock for the citizens of the East when everything changed so drastically and quickly. It wouldn't have helped in the transition period being treated as inferior by some of the inhabitants of West Berlin/West Germany.

On a visit to Berlin in 2016 I was standing waiting to cross the road at the Yorckstrasse/Mehringdamm crossing (West Berlin) when a car raced past, possibly just before the lights changed to red. A woman standing next to me turned and said, "These stupid Easties (Ossies) they don't know how to drive." I was completely shocked by this as there was no way the woman could have known whether the driver was from the East, West or even Middle Earth. As far as this woman was concerned it had to be someone from the East because in her eyes they were responsible for anything negative and probably nobody could convince her otherwise.

Slow build up to Wall opening

When you have that kind of ingrained, small mindedness it isn't perhaps surprising that a gulf between the East and West still exists.

Thirty years after the Wall crumbled one of the many divisions still existing between East and West is financial. I was shocked to discover that people in the East are being paid less for doing exactly the same job as their counterparts employed in the West. I was also really amazed to discover that the people have accepted such an unfair situation for so long. Why would any fair country pay some people less than others for doing the same job?

There was a strike of tram drivers in Leipzig in 2018 and the reason for their strike was that they were being paid less than tram drivers in the West. It isn't only tram drivers who are exploited in this way. If you are a Social Worker for example who had been an East citizen and had done your training there then you could end up being paid less because you don't have "acceptable" Diplomas regardless of whether you have been doing the same job as your West German colleagues for twenty or thirty years. (Diplomas and similar from the East were always viewed as inferior to those obtained in the West). The Germans in general appear to place huge importance on Diplomas whereas experience and personality seem less relevant.

The resentment which some former East German citizens feel towards the West Berlin/German Government can be understood. There is resentment about the way their country was bought, trashed and pillaged in many ways by rich West German individuals and companies who bought going concerns

Slow build up to Wall opening

in the East for a pittance and then promptly closed some of them down to destroy any possibility of competition.

On a visit to Berlin and Germany in 2018 I couldn't help but notice the similarity in the way the former East Germans are (still) treated by many in the West and the way in which the Scottish people have been treated by the English/British Government and some English people since the so-called "Union" of 1707. There is definitely the same arrogant superior attitude displayed by some in the West towards those in the East.

The Ministry of Fear

Nothing appears more surprising to those, who consider human affairs with a philosophical eye, than the easiness with which the many are governed by the few; and the implicit submission, with which men resign their own sentiments and passions to those of their rulers. David Hume

The Ministry for State Security, better known as the Stasi (secret police) created an atmosphere of fear which is how most Governments control their citizens because the more your life is driven by fear the easier you are to control. It's estimated that many citizens of the East were spying on each other. How could you trust someone again, maybe a spouse or family member if you discovered they had been reporting your every word and move, even your private thoughts to the State police? Not an easy one to deal with.

After it was clear that the GDR was dead and gone the Stasi started to destroy the thousands of secret files they held on people but were prevented from destroying them all by enraged East German citizens who stormed their offices.

There are so many files involved that the authorities still haven't been able to go through them all and inform those who have a file (part of) its content. Some of the information in the report you receive is redacted so that you are not given the full story. It is suspected that a number of the staff entrusted with this work were former Stasi members or informants (which seems a bit like getting the fox to guard the henhouse) you wonder how much information has been redacted in order to protect them and others like them? The fact that the German government has cut funding for the staff carrying out this work isn't going to speed up the process in any way. Common sense would dictate that you increase the staff doing this to get the job done quicker. Perhaps there are ulterior motives for the delay?

In 2018 I decided to enquire whether the Stasi had a file on me. I don't know why I hadn't done it sooner. I was actually prompted to do so by my former colleague in the British Embassy, Claudia Linde. The joint boss we had at that time was apparently so lacking in common sense that he travelled around the East in his spare time approaching East Germans in the search for information about supposed relatives he was seeking. He soon caught the attention of the Stasi with his irresponsible behaviour. I surmised that they perhaps had a file on me as well if they had him under surveillance although they perhaps automatically had files on all foreigners who lived or worked in the East.

I had also met an East German Artist through my work and he and his wife invited me to visit them in their home. I did this a few times but it wasn't a case of driving to their house which was in a rural setting. The artist asked me to drive to Potsdam and park my car there. We then met up in the town and he drove me to his home. So who knows whether I had been followed by the Stasi.

I have been informed that yes I do have a Stasi file but I won't be able to see what is in it for a couple of years (due to the above mentioned "staff shortage").

Who owns the Wall?

You would think it would be perfectly clear who owned a huge Wall which was 1.3km long over 3m high and pretty difficult to overlook but surprisingly that wasn't the case in 1990. The Border Guards were the Custodians of the Wall whilst it was still part of the official GDR border but it was owned by the National Defence Ministry. Friedrichshain Council however didn't seem to be aware of this as our experience with them demonstrated.

Diary entries 3.9.90

Back to 12 hour days. Heading for the opening of ESG on 28.9. Trying to get the contract signed and things organised in the East is still a nightmare.

5.9.90
Fuerchner (Friedrichshain) runs around all day trying to ascertain who owns the Wall.

6.9.90
08.00 At Fuerchner's office we are handed two letters which confirm that Friedrichshain now own the Wall.
09.00 meeting with obnoxious idiot at Friedrichshain who won't sign the new contract with wuva and who said no decision could be made until 24/9 - four days before opening.
16.00 After discussion at wuva's office we are back at Fuerchner's who arranges a meeting with Friedrichshain for Monday 10.9. at 13.00.

Depression gets us all – no motivation as things are uncertain.
7-9.9.90 Weekend.

Who owns the Wall?

I finally get some time off again. Was briefly in the office Sat &
Sun with Peter(Nagelschmidt) but neither of us had much
motivation. I slept a lot Sunday.

There is a perception that artists have huge egos and can be
difficult to deal with. I can't say that characteristic is more
prevalent among artists than the rest of the population but a
few of the East Side Gallery artists certainly fell into that
category. I was "befriended" by some people who thought that
getting close to me was going to further their goals or get them
into the limelight. I was too naïve to notice it at the time.

In addition to looking after the artists I became the person who
ended up giving interviews to the world media. I think mostly
this happened because I was there, on the spot and the media
often turned up at any time. Once you give a few interviews it
then seems to become self perpetuating. By August a large
number of positive press and media reports had built up and
then along came Karlin Wolf, an extremely unpleasant woman
who changed all that. She wasn't an East Side Gallery artist but
was in a relationship with one, the Italian, Fulvio Pinna
(Fortunately for him, in my opinion, the man is now married to
someone else). I don't know what motivated her it may have
been greed, envy, the need for power, who knows. What I do
know is that she very quickly stirred up a negative Press. She
got together with five Russian Artists via their Manager,
Brodowski and claimed to represent five others (including
Fulvio) and was implying that the Artists weren't being treated
fairly. She falsely claimed to be the representative of all the
East Side Gallery artists instead of a maximum of ten.

Who owns the Wall?

Diary entries

26.9.90
The "unpleasant one" is at it again. She sent a letter full of false information to many of the artists and arranged a meeting at her place.

27.9.90
Rainer, Peter and I are eating at Strada when Mark and Maja bring news that we are wanted at the meeting. It's been a difficult day, overtired, tension high. I don't have any energy anymore and have to go home. The last night before the opening there is still so much to do.

One of the left-wing papers in Berlin printed Karlin Wolf's story without checking with wuva or I whether there was any basis to her allegations. This was one of my first experiences of very poor journalism and complete bias which has made me doubt most things in the Press every since.

There is now much more (although still not enough) awareness of the bias and propaganda of the mainstream Press. The media often functions as the voice of the Government and broadcasts whatever the Government of the day wants us to hear (certainly the case in Britain currently) but that example and others where I was falsely described in articles as a former Ambassador, a London Gallery owner etc was the point at which I realised you couldn't believe most of what you read or hear in the media. When you actually gave an interview to a journalist other than them copying what someone else had written, they still rarely got it right.

Make it historic

Long before the Gallery was completed in September 1990 wuva applied to the Berlin authorities to have the Gallery declared a Historic Monument. Not only did this part of the Wall form part of the actual border installation between East and West but it had now been transformed into a Gallery by 118 international artists.

One Scottish newspaper article on the Gallery carried the heading "Healing the Wall Wounded," which I found very appropriate. It really was about transformation. It was a reversal of usage as the Wall was no longer keeping people apart but uniting them. The "messages" broadcast by the Wall before 1989 were those of fear, intimidation and control and after it was painted the messages were more about love, peace, hope, the desire for a better future and togetherness.

East Side Gallery was declared a Historic Monument in November 1991. It was assumed that this would save the Gallery from partial or complete destruction but as we know, this is sadly not what happened.

The official opening

Diary entry

28.9.90 'D' Day
The opening. Having great problems to cope, just exhausted. Have to pull myself together to get through today. Kikue and Günther arrive about 11.00 I leave at 12 for the Wall. Still some painters working at the last moment. Walked from the end of the Gallery over the bridge to the boat. Mary Mackey was there having problems communicating with the crew.

16.30 meeting on the Oberbaumbrücke, the mayor of Friedrichshain, Mendiburu turns up. It was nice to meet all the artists.

17.00 we start walking the length of the Gallery supposed to be bussed back but the buses didn't turn up.

18.00 on the boat met by the drummer group that was really nice. I had to do the opening speech. I told them I wasn't happy about standing in front of them. I was so relieved when it was all over then I started to enjoy the evening. Peter, Maja, Mark, Mary and I and a few others went on to the Bronx (club) and it was 4 am when I got home. It was a good night.

We had originally planned to have the official opening of the East Side Gallery on August 13th 1990 which would have been the 29th anniversary of the Wall going up. As things don't often go to plan that is exactly what happened. They didn't. The main reason was that Friedrichshain Council were just mucking us about and still hadn't issued wuva with a new contract which wuva rightly felt was important. There were some spaces on the Gallery which were still blank and some artists were still painting the day before and even on the day of the opening. The whole project was like an ebb and flow anyway. There were times when there weren't enough artists, we were short of paint, or some artists changed their mind. One moment all the slots had been allocated to someone and then they may have needed a smaller space than initially envisaged and so we found ourselves with empty spaces.

The 28th September was then decided upon for the official opening and as there were no suitable buildings near the Gallery which we could use for a function we hired a boat which was moored at the other (west) side of the Oberbaum bridge on the river Spree. The bridge was still closed to traffic at that time so we walked across it. Now, with so many openings in the Gallery it is possible to get behind it onto the riverbank but that wasn't possible then as the Gallery was still intact and there was no access.

All the artists were invited to the opening, a band was hired and food and drink supplied for everyone. We had asked Michail Gorbachow and Willi Brandt (former West German Chancellor) if either of them would officiate but both declined. We then asked another "important" person who also declined so it was left for me to open proceedings. I prefer not to be in the spotlight therefore I wasn't too happy about it but that is the way it turned out.

The Germans call something which is cheap Schottenpreis (Scottish price) probably stemming from the myth that Scots are tight with their money. I know few nationalities which are more generous than the Scots and that isn't someone talking through bias. However, the Scots are *careful* with their money. They don't tend to waste it or throw it away and can often achieve a lot with a little. I recall making a joke about this at the opening. I said if a German had been managing and co-creating the East Side Gallery and not a Scot then it may never have come to be because that Scots canniness and ability to make do with whatever is at hand and to work without a plan was instrumental in the creation of the East Side Gallery.

Diary entry

26.10.90
What's been happening – had to come back from holiday early because of all the happenings here Wolf & Brodowski are now trying to buy the Wall.

We have an artists' meeting on 9th November followed by video clips of ESG shown by Walter, (a friend of one of the artists who took videos of some of the artists at work) a jazz band and a (hopefully) short question and answer session.
Apart from that things are in a state of total limbo.
Friedrichshain are pissing wuva around something terrible.

Plenary meeting

On November 9th 1990 a plenary meeting of the artists was called. One of the items on the agenda was the electing of an Artists committee which would in future represent the artists and guarantee their right to have a say in all matters concerning the Gallery. There were 37 of the artists present. Eight who couldn't attend had submitted their written authorisation so that a total of 45 voting rights were available (there were 118 ESG artists in total).

At that point it was still unclear what was going to happen to the East Side Gallery; whether it could stay on its original site or it had to be removed, as neither Friedrichshain Council nor the Berlin Senate were capable of making any binding decisions. Nor were these same authorities able to clear the legal status of who owned ESG. It was noted that this was due to the ignorance and delaying tactics of the Politicians responsible. Apart from the obvious reason, it was explained to those present at the meeting that clarity about the legal status was necessary as reassurance for possible sponsors and it would also enable immediate steps to be taken to protect the Gallery. Another item on the agenda was the financial situation which showed that the total outgoings were 252,804.92 DM and the total income 108,935.30 DM.

Artists Committee

The first Artists committee was elected on November 9th 1990 as with the Gallery now complete and the plans by the Senate to tear it down discarded, how it was looked after in the future became an important issue. All of the East Side Gallery artists were eligible to become members.

Plenary meeting

As mentioned above, even just after the Gallery opened there were only 45 people interested enough to vote. For some of the artists the Gallery was perhaps just another project they took part in when they were young but in which they had no further interest after its completion. In 1996 an Artists Initiative (*Künstlerinitiative East Side Gallery *e.V.*) was founded under the chairmanship of Kani Alavi. However, at no time has the Artists Initiative spoken for nor represented all the East Side Gallery artists. In 2011 another Artists Initiative was founded under the name *East Side Gallery International – Seoul e.V.*

*e.V – registered association

East Side story

The following is a press release which the author and wuva released on 10.11.1990.

"East Side Story"

or

"The controlling hand of the authorities"

wuva and Christine MacLean found each other at the beginning of April. They were both dissatisfied in their different ways, wuva with their idea and Christine with her working partner. Thus began the joint, enthusiastic project "East Side Gallery, on the section of the Wall in Mühlenstrasse. Wuva, presented the concept for a gallery to Friedrichshain Council in order to amend the original contract which was for advertising. At the same time, wuva and Christine MacLean sought interest and support among the freshly elected leaders of *SPD, CDU and PDS none of whom replied. Only Herr Tragsdorf from Friedrichshain Council contacted us in the middle of April to inform us that nobody would be making any decisions before the elections.

That was however a huge understatement because decisions never were made.

*SPD/CDU/PDS – Political parties

By the way, during this time one mural after the other had appeared on the Wall and the world media had long since become "family friends" at the gallery.

East Side story

The following months can be read in telegram style as follows:

May

wuva endeavours to secure the long-term location of the gallery.

The municipal architect, Frau Richter cannot guarantee the current location of the Gallery till the end of 1990. We can probably reckon with the dismantling of it in the summer.

The idea for the world tour arises in order to guarantee the future survival of the gallery.

June

Friedrichshain Council send us to the Magistrat as it was discovered that they (Friedrichshain) are not legally responsible for the Wall.

July 18

Finally a meeting with the new mayor of the Friedrichshain district. Conclusion: sympathetic approval but the competency lies with the city Mayor.

July/Aug

Extensive exchange of correspondence and dozens of talks with the Magistrat, Authorities and Ministries which were inconclusive, forcing wuva to postpone the planned gallery opening on 13.8.90.

Sept 6.9.90 – the day arrives at last!

Successful process wuva – Monty. Wuva is successful in their court case against Monty who was making claims that he was still the operator of the gallery.

East Side story

In a letter from the Ministry for Disarmament and Defence the legal entity is transferred to Friedrichshain Council putting into effect the option to secure the project East Side Gallery and its development.

With that, to all intents and purposes, the state of play reverted to how it was in April except the gallery was now almost complete with a contract for the new situation still nowhere in sight.

New draft contracts were altered and rewritten time and time again. The men from Friedrichshain Council had new demands and requests on a weekly basis and wuva agreed to all of them not least because time was running out.

The Gallery opening finally took place on 28th September 1990 in the presence of the mayor of Friedrichshain but without an official contract.

By the way, the final draft version of the contract contained the following demands from Friedrichshain Council:

- Removal of the gallery within 6 months of signing the contract
- The erection of a metal fence with concrete supports where the gallery stood
- The erection of fences at right angles to the river
- Levelling of the land behind the Wall
- Dismantling of all remains of the border installation including watchtowers, concrete posts, Wall pieces etc
- Reclamation of and planting of the land

This was all to be carried out at the expense of wuva and the artists. In addition a guaranteed 25% of the total turnover from the project was to be paid to the Council.

On the day after the official opening of the gallery, at the instigation of the art manager Karlin Wolf (partner of the Italian painter Fulvio Pinna who lived in West Berlin) a meeting of the artists took place to which Frau Wolf had also invited the mayor of Friedrichshain. The speculation with regard to the development of the gallery contained in the letter she had circulated was hereby disproven.

The result of the meeting in which around 30 artists participated was the unanimous decision that arrangements were to be made by wuva to call a plenary meeting of the artists on 9th November with the aim of arranging a democratically elected artists committee.

Despite this the art Manager, Frau Wolf-Tepas and Herr Brodowski (Brodowski was the manager of five Russian artists) arranged several meetings with a handful of people before the 9th November without the knowledge of the gallery operator and as the so-called "Wall painters interest group Mühlen-strasse" applied to the Senate and Council on 15.10.90 for a purchase option for the gallery and the security of the self-determination by the artists and sparked a Press campaign against wuva "in the name of all the artists." This led, among other things, to Friedrichshain Council ignoring the last version of the contract as listed above and declaring to wuva that there was no longer any need for action.

East Side story

According to Frau Wolf on the day of the plenary meeting, the Interest Group amounted to 14 people despite one of the artists at the plenary meeting declaring that she had not signed and was not joining the group although her name was already on the list of the "Interest Group Mühlenstrasse." The East Side Gallery was created by 118 artists (long live democracy)!

The last talk with Friedrichshain Council took place with Herr Winkler on the pre-arranged date of 10th October as the mayor had no intention of meeting wuva again.

A session of the Council took place on 15.10 and wuva only found out about the content of the meeting a few days later when it was published in the *taz* newspaper.

Meanwhile the District Assembly met with the result that everything stays as it was.

However the Council is of the firm opinion that only the relevant architects and the Senate can decide the fate of the gallery.

Viewed from today's perspective, the Wall could still be there for several years. A firm decision on the future of the gallery is not expected for two or three years after the architects have submitted their respective development plans.

The question arises as to whether the current mayor, Herr Helios Mendiburu and his crew ever had a plan of action with regard to wuva and the gallery especially as he insinuated publically several times that this firm is one of those disreputable limited companies which profited from the former (East German) state....

It is well known however that slander and speculation are a distraction and well exploited in electoral campaigns.

Wuva and Christine MacLean would like once again to refer to the fact that the art managers Herr Brodowski and Frau Wolf started an artists' interest group whose apparent aim is to market and sell some of the works without informing and without the consent of the artists. This conclusion is derived from the Press information whose source is obvious. In this regard Frau MacLean and wuva reserve the right to take legal action.

In contrast to this, genuine democratic steps and results arose from the artist's plenary meeting on 9th November in which 45 artists participated.

The artists committee was selected by a majority using individual votes. The modus operandi of the manager Frau Wolf was rejected and the arrogant claim that the so-called "interest group" spoke on behalf of all artists" denounced. In addition, the Committee was entrusted with the founding of a Trust for the promotion of artistic projects and the distribution of the revenues. Finally the majority of the artists who were present were in favour of discussing questions and problems among all parties and not to settle these via the Media.

East Side story

All artists who didn't participate in this process were given until December to express their views on the suggested principles of the work and the project as discussed in the plenary meeting.

Wuva, Miss MacLean and the majority of those present on November 9th are acting on the assumption that the East Side Gallery arose in and belongs to this city. We hope that the city fathers will allocate a permanent location for the gallery very soon.

Note from author: How would things have turned out if the Artists Committee had as intended, founded an East Side Gallery Trust in 1990/1991?

Let's come together - reunification

The reunification of the two Germanys had of course to be made official. This rubber stamping of the (re)new(ed) country took place on 3rd October 1990 and is now known as the day of German Unity. A Unification Treaty between the Federal Republic of Germany (FRG) and the Democratic Republic of Germany (GDR) was signed on 31st August 1990 and this effectively dissolved the GDR and confirmed its accession to the FRG. Just like that.

After one Germany was created a "Solidarity tax" was introduced by Helmut Kohl, the Chancellor at that time. This tax was supposed to be temporary but it still exists today. The purpose of the Solidarity tax was to help rebuild the East. Thirty years on and many ask what that money is now being spent on. Some residents in the former west part of Berlin would argue that it is time to spend some money on the infrastructure in the West.

The quiet after the storm

After the Gallery was completed and the official opening was behind us one of the most important things I did was catch up on sleep. Prior to that I would never have believed that you could actually do that, but you can, because I did. I had been working long days, seven days a week for many weeks prior to the completion of the Gallery and exhaustion had now taken over.

There were lots of conflicting thoughts going through my head during that time such as, "Why on earth did I get involved in the project? Was it really worth giving up a year of my life for?" The obstacles that were put in our way by the authorities and the problems and negative press caused by a handful of people made me really wonder. Around Christmas time in 1990 I went to the Gallery and just walked along its length, something I had done so many times throughout that year. There were still busloads of people from many Nations coming to view the Gallery often dodging the traffic to cross from the other side where their buses had parked. I found their presence reassuring in a way, a form of confirmation that it *was* of value, it *was* worth it. If the Gallery attracted crowds of hundreds, thousands and over time, millions of people then I reasoned that it was perhaps after all a project worth doing.

Catalogue

In 1991 wuva commissioned a catalogue for the Gallery from Oberbaum Verlag (Publisher) in Berlin intending for it to be issued in August of that year. The East German photographer Rita May was engaged to photograph both the artists and their paintings. The catalogue was to contain a brief story as to how the East Side Gallery had been created as well as biographies and photos of all the artists and everyone involved in the project.

When a sample catalogue was received for proof reading there were mistakes in my biography and that of Rainer's and several of the artists had no biography or photo. The entire story of East Side Gallery was missing and no Sponsors were listed so the proofs were returned to the publishers and they were instructed not to print until the necessary corrections were carried out. Unfortunately, none of the corrections was made and an incomplete catalogue with many omissions and several mistakes was issued.

Diary entry 12.9.91

The Oberbaum Verlag issued a catalogue full of omissions. The Verlag was supposed to sign a new Agreement with wuva regarding corrections etc but never met the appointment.

In 1991 in an attempt to fill the gap, I wrote a small booklet about the creation process of the Gallery. I had it published in German and English and reprinted the English version in 2017. The story had never been told and I felt it important to get something out there, however brief.

New adventures

My official association with the East Side Gallery ceased in the summer of 1991 when I took a part-time job elsewhere although I still had some involvement such as organising biographies and photos for the catalogue and dealing with correspondence. My main task had been the co-ordination of the artists' work and supporting them with their painting. In the autumn of 1991 wuva was in a shaky position financially and had moved to new office premises.

Towards the end of 1991 I hitched a lift to Romania in a bullet-proof Mercedes with my new employer and colleagues who were Lebanese, or so I thought. We stopped overnight during the long car journey to Romania and I was sent in to prospective hotels to enquire about rooms. I didn't think anything of it at the time but now of course I realise that having someone with a British Passport ask for rooms was very advantageous to them.

My year in Romania was one of the best of my life. The people shared the little they had. I learnt Romanian very quickly. The fact that there was no access to TV or media in English meant I had the ideal opportunity to immerse myself in the language and as most Romanians didn't speak English the desire to communicate motivated me to learn quickly.

After my year in Romania I moved to Leverkusen for a couple of years returning to Scotland at the end of 1995.

I spent a further four years in Berlin from 2006-2010 before again returning to Scotland.

The great renovation

As you can imagine, the Gallery is completely unprotected from people scribbling their names on it or from destroying entire paintings. It is extremely difficult to protect something so big which is in the public domain. Many ideas have been thrown about over the years as to how to protect the paintings from damage by the public. Some of the more bizarre suggestions were erecting a fence in front of the Wall/Gallery which is really perverse when you think about it.

None of the Berlin authorities had ever supported the East Side Gallery in any shape or form and actually caused us many headaches and a great deal of stress during the creation of the Gallery.

The Berlin Senate never paid a penny for the Gallery, (that's right, it cost them nothing, the Gallery was funded by wuva). The Authorities treated the Gallery like a rotting potato which they batted back and fore for 28 years. They had no appreciation of the huge historical and cultural significance of the East Side Gallery. The importance of the Gallery was recognised by the rest of the world but the Berlin Senate couldn't seem to grasp that.

In 2009 the Berlin Senate paid out around 3 Million Euros for the renovation of the Gallery. This covered the cost of repairing the Wall and paying each artist 3,000 Euros to repaint their murals. By this time it was structurally as well as visibly in a dreadful state as people had been chipping bits out of it for souvenirs.

The great renovation

You might wonder why the Senate all of a sudden had became so generous but the reason was certainly not altruistic. The year 2009 was the 20th anniversary of the opening of the Wall and the Senate probably noticed that the Wall was still a very powerful draw for people so they decided to clean it up.

The Wall at that point was taken right back to its bare metal supports and then rebuilt. It is a bit ironic when you think about it. One minute everyone wants to tear down the Wall, the next it is being rebuilt.

When you consider that the artists were not paid for their work the first time around the 3,000 Euros they received for the repainting was a big improvement. A company called *S.T.E.R.N. Ltd* was engaged by the Berlin Senate to oversee the project and pay the artists. Several unemployed people were engaged (probably for a very low wage) as part of a Government job creation scheme to support the artists by carrying equipment and paint and assisting as required. This was certainly a very welcome support when you consider that several of the artists had become senior citizens. The working conditions were a complete contrast to those in 1990 not least because none of it took place in winter but also because of the help the artists received.

Some of the artists were dead by then and others had no further interest in repainting so a small self-selected group of East Side Gallery artists renovated a number of these paintings in addition to their own and collected 3,000 Euros for each one. The same artist could be observed working on several paintings. In at least one case, there was very little effort made to find the artist to give them the opportunity to redo their work and this time round to be financially rewarded for it. One artist, Lance Keller who had painted the cover of Pink Floyd's record *The Wall* as well as Oskar's drawing of the Brandenburg Gate was actually declared dead because, as Jörg Weber, the Press officer for the Artists Initiative later told me, "He wasn't at his previous address" A short while after I was told this I went to the Residents Registration Office, paid 5 Euros and received Lance's new address.

Two artists refused to repaint their murals and would not allow anyone else to redo their work because they wanted more money than was being offered. Their spaces remain blank to this day.

The artist Jim Avignon didn't agree with painting the same mural over and over again so he didn't take part in the renovation in 2009. Instead Jim came along one evening in 2013 and created a brand new painting which annoyed some people and pleased others.

When the great renovation took place in 2009 small plaques were erected in front of the paintings and this would have been an ideal opportunity to honour David Monty as the initiator of the Gallery but that didn't happen.

All the murals were repainted at least once throughout the years some several times. Artists who lived locally would often repair their mural at their own expense and some paintings were repainted by members of the Artists Initiative without the permission of the original artist.

The great renovation

Ultimately it became impossible to repaint as the "canvas" was disappearing at the hands of "Wall hackers" determined to take home a piece of the Wall. The exception to this is the painting entitled "Hands" a joint venture between the Scots Margaret Hunter and Peter Russell. This painting is the only original painting from 1990 as instead of Margaret and Peter repainting it in 2009 it was professionally restored. It has since been neglected and left to deteriorate.

Public art is always going to be copied and photographed but some of the East Side Gallery artists found their work being marketed or used in advertising without their permission and with no remuneration being paid to them. The East Side Gallery artists had signed a contract giving wuva the marketing rights for their work for a period of five years ie to September 28th 1995 at the latest. After that time the marketing rights returned to the artist. However, one artist who pursued a company for using his artwork without permission discovered that the company had paid money to the "East Side Gallery" and had thus falsely assumed they could use his painting in their advertising campaign. So somebody named the "East Side Gallery" is taking money from companies to which they are not entitled, money which belongs to the artist.

The film

It was in 2009 that filmmaker duo Dirk Szuszies and Karin Kaper got involved in the making of a film about the East Side Gallery at the suggestion of a friend. They filmed most of the artists during the grand renovation and beyond. I was back living in Berlin at that point but had had no official function with the running of the Gallery since mid 1991.

Neither Dirk nor Karin was aware of the role that Monty and I had played in the creation of the Gallery. It was thanks to artists Margaret Hunter and Mary Mackey that we appeared in the film. It was at this point that I decided to write this book to present the facts about how the East Side Gallery came into being as it was obvious that several people were making completely false claims about being co-founders of the Gallery.

The Film was premiered in the Babylon Cinema, Berlin Mitte on 6th January 2015. It was at the premiere that I met Monty again for the first time in twenty-five years. I was really pleased to connect with him again and happy for him that he was finally gaining some of the recognition and respect due to him for being the person who had brought the East Side Gallery into being. The DVD of the film was released in 2019.

The destructive phase

The Gallery had suffered acts of vandalism from the very beginning, primarily at the hands of tourists. It usually took the form of writing their names on the paintings, you know, the usual, "xyz was here." Initially the damage was pretty minor but through time some even drew or spray painted over the murals. There was a particularly bad incident in late 1991 as several paintings were almost completely obliterated when sprayed with dark green paint. The culprits, who quite openly owned up to it, were never prosecuted.

However, in 1996 the Gallery experienced the first act of vandalism sanctioned by the Authorities. In November 1996 the Berlin Lower Monument office granted permission for an opening to be made in the Wall to enable vehicles to access the plot at 78-80 Mühlenstrasse (at the beginning of the gallery) which at that time housed a club in a former Silo. This should never have happened and possibly set the precedent for the further acts of vandalism which were approved by the State. A gap in the Wall suitable for vehicles already existed next to the small building used as a shop which wasn't far from the club. This had allowed the GDR military and their vehicles access to the rear of the Wall.

As a result of this official approval the entire section of Wall painted by the Japanese Painter Kikue Miyatake was removed to create the access to the former Silo which was built in 1907 originally to store grain. The granary, due to its exposed location at the edge of the river Spree behind the East Side Gallery was incorporated into the border by the GDR regime and used as a lookout point.

The destructive phase

They built a watchtower on top of it from where anyone attempting to escape to the West could be easily spotted. After the demise of the GDR the former Granary was turned into a club.

The sections which were removed were placed behind the Gallery at the side of the Granary where they were easy prey for vandals and spray painters. They were still in that location in 2009 when Kikue renovated her painting yet again.

The state sanctioned vandalism continued in 2006 when an American businessman named Anschutz was permitted to create an opening in the East Side Gallery so that people could come by boat to the O2 concert hall (now Mercedes-Benz Arena) which he was having constructed nearby. There were huge protests by many Berliners but this didn't prevent another permanent break in the Wall.

The sections which were removed 'Die Masken', by artist Slawa, were again placed behind the Wall where they were of course open to vandalism by souvenir hunters.

Broken laws and missing files

The next part in the destructive phase was in 2013 when over 90,000 signed a Petition to prevent another permanent opening in the Gallery and subsequent building of the *Living Levels*, so-called luxury flats on the former death strip. Building within a specified distance of a listed monument is illegal under § 10 of the Protected Monument Law, nothing can change that fact. It is inexcusable that illegal building in close proximity to the Gallery has been permitted. It should be a source of acute embarrassment to the Berlin Government that such construction has been sanctioned. In Berlin it would seem to depend on who makes the application for planning permission as to whether this Law is enforced or not.

Regrettably the petition, despite Roger Waters of Pink Floyd making a personal appearance at the Gallery and adding his voice to those opposed to its destruction for purely commercial gain, did not prevent the development going ahead. The German Developer, Maik Uwe Hinkel, had allegedly been an "unofficial informant" for the Stasi which added to the anger and indignation of the public.

Joerg Bereths, at that time a member of the group 'Save East Side Gallery!' went to the Land Registry on May 16th 2013 to inspect the records for the construction projects at Mühlenstrasse 60 and 61-63. To his astonishment the registration official told him that the electronic entries for the *Living Levels* development at Number 60, without which the land register pages could not be assigned, had been deleted. She also pointed out that such deletions could only be made by someone with a high level of authority.

Broken laws and missing files

When questioned about it she explained that this was totally unheard of and that she had no explanation for this deletion.

Apart from this being highly irregular in Germany it raises the question as to why it was deemed necessary to delete it and who would have had the authority to do so?

Wall included in price

After the Second World War land and property which had been confiscated was reclaimed. This was, for obvious reasons, not possible when the land was incorporated into the East German border installation. This changed when the Wall came down and meant that there were several landowners along the 1.3km length of the Gallery keen to regain their property. Owning land on the former death strip also gave them possession of the Wall segments standing on their plot, a situation I find bizarre.

Petition time again

In 2018 another Petition which was supported by the actor David Hasselhoff, was started to prevent the building of the monstrous *Pier 61/63* Hotel complex again on the former death strip. The Developer this time, the Israeli, Haeskel Nathaniel with his company Trockland Ltd, had allegedly also been a member of a secret police force. There must be something about the energy of the former death strip which attracts such types. It could be seen as ironic if it wasn't so morally repugnant.

Initially *Pier 61/63* was for a 7 storey hotel but the Berlin Mayor at that time, Klaus Wowereit "gave" the Developer another two floors on condition that the *Living Levels* development and the *Pier 61/63* Hotel complex share one entrance (opening) in the Gallery when the *Pier 61/63* monstrosity is completed. Let us see if that actually happens. It is written into their contract but as we have already witnessed with contracts and historical monument status in Berlin, nobody gives a damn and greed seems to be the motive for most of the players.

Disinterest and downright sabotage played a big part in the failure of this petition. The mayor of Berlin, Michael Müller didn't even bother to reply to correspondence asking for him to do something. Nor did he reply to our request to accept delivery of the petition so he obviously wasn't going to intervene in any way. Mr Müller has a reputation for not replying to Berlin citizens if he doesn't want to. That isn't democracy, not that we are under the illusion that Berliners are living in a democracy. There aren't many democracies around.

Petition time again

The petition was sabotaged when a member of the group 'Save the East Side Gallery!' who had launched the petition presented himself to the media as a spokesperson for the group, despite having officially left the Group a few weeks earlier. He informed the media that the Activists had made a deal with the Developer. He perhaps had, but the majority of the others for whom he falsely claimed to speak hadn't.

So, the next and supposedly final removal of Wall segments happened in 2018, again at the behest of the Berlin Senate

A Monument to Joy

It was the East Side Gallery film which prompted the founding members of the group, 'Monument to Joy' Joerg Bereths and Thomas Rojahn to contact me in late 2015.

Joerg and Thomas felt that the East Side Gallery should be declared a living Monument to Joy as joy had been the prevailing emotion when the Wall was opened and their feeling was that the Gallery embodied this essence. I thought that was a great idea.

Joerg and Thomas felt it was important that the East Side Gallery wasn't turned into a dead museum piece but was a place of action and life thus a 'living' monument

How many monuments to Joy are there in the world? The world certainly needs more joy. There are so many monuments or memorials to conflict and terror but not one of these has prevented mankind from committing further acts of terror or starting wars. A Monument to Joy is an excellent idea. Surely it is far more ethical and desirable to promote and spread joy than fear and terror. Let us not forget that emotions are contagious. Wouldn't it be great to infect the millions of yearly visitors to the East Side Gallery with joy?

Joy – a feeling of deep happiness, pleasure contentment. What a lovely thing to wish someone.

A Monument to Joy

Joerg Bereths

When I recall the pictures of the night the Wall fell I see pictures of absolute joy. I see complete strangers, spontaneously embracing each other. I see fountains of sekt and people wildly drumming on Trabi roofs. At the same time I also recall the images of the students on "Tiananmen Square", who were less fortunate, as well as pictures of a long human chain across the Baltic States.

A deep longing an ancient dream of humanity became a reality for me for a few hours on the night the Berlin Wall fell; a longing that so far only Schiller has been able to express in

A Monument to Joy

words in relation to Beethoven's 'Ode to Joy': On that night in the presence of joy, people who were complete strangers suddenly acted as sisters and brothers. As a result of this joy, it was irrelevant where you came from, which class you belonged to or which "fashion" you were beholden to.

I've thought long and hard about what kind of fascination has caused me to fight for the fate of the East Side Gallery for the past six years. In addition to the encouragement of my fellow campaigners* Chris MacLean and Thomas (Tomek) Rojahn, for me it was a specific recognition: the "Spirit of the Year 1989" and the 'Ode to Joy' along the East Side Gallery became manifest in 1990 through the work of 118 international artists. In this respect, the East Side Gallery is for me a place where the joy on the night of the Fall of the Berlin Wall must remain particularly tangible. Despite the fact that the East Side Gallery has meanwhile become the property of the Berlin Wall Foundation, in my opinion this place still cries out for joy in accordance with the concept of a living monument: East Side Gallery – 'A Living Monument to Joy!'

Joerg Bereths

A Monument to Joy

Thomas Rojahn

<u>For me the East Side Gallery represents joy.</u>

I associate the Gallery with the joy that prevailed that evening and Beethoven's 9th Symphony 'Ode to Joy,' when the Wall which divided not only Germany but two hostile systems was overcome. You only have to recall the images of the night the Berlin Wall fell. I somehow envisage the moment that Schiller and Beethoven wanted to express being like this or similar. A utopian moment in which the human family united

A Monument to Joy

After the Fall of the Berlin Wall, there was justifiable hope for peaceful coexistence in Europe and the world. However, the strategy of change through rapprochement or cooperation instead of confrontation has now reverted to the opposite.

It is therefore important to preserve the East Side Gallery as a monument for future generations.

As a symbol of international understanding, the East Side Gallery should encourage people to work for the overcoming of walls, for freedom and peace. Freedom is not a gift, you have to struggle for it time and again. Therefore the Gallery should not be a static museum piece but a living monument, 'A living monument to joy'.

Since the East Side Gallery was also a street art project, the focus of the work is art. Since art can speak in metaphors for me it is the ideal means to imbue the Gallery with life in the sense of the monument's main message.

Thomas Rojahn

A Monument to Joy

Joerg and Thomas were very active in promoting the East Side Gallery as a Monument to Joy. On October 13th 2017 a Hearing entitled "First steps towards developing a comprehensive concept for the future of the East Side Gallery" took place in the Friedrichshain-Kreuzberg Museum, Berlin. Thomas Rojahn together with some friends built a copy of some segments of the Wall and then arranged for them to be painted. These segments were installed in the grounds of the Museum on the day of the Hearing.

The Berlin Senate was planning to hand the East Side Gallery over to the Berlin Wall Foundation and there was doubt among many present at the Hearing that the Foundation was the appropriate custodian.

For over four hours varying opinions as to possible futures for the Gallery were expressed by several parties with different agendas. Professor Klausmeier, the Director of the Berlin Wall Foundation stated that if (when) the Foundation took control of the East Side Gallery then he would be following the Historic Monument Law to the letter and that the Foundation alone would make the decisions. This statement intensified the reservations voiced at the meeting about the Foundation's suitability as a custodian of the East Side Gallery because the Gallery didn't fit into existing Historic Monument criteria.

Berlin Wall Foundation

The Foundation plays a very important role in the maintenance of original sections of the Berlin Wall in Bernauer Strasse as a reminder of man's inhumanity to man. It is important to have such reminders. The East Side Gallery however is a symbol of transformation.

The negative emanation of the Wall on Mühlenstrasse has been changed forever by the positive input of the artists and all those involved in the creation of the Gallery. It cannot be compared to the pieces of Wall on Bernauer Strasse and it must not become a dead museum. The East Side Gallery needs to be respected for what it is; both a monument to man's gross stupidity and cruelty and as an object of hope as to how something can be overcome and transformed.

One of the plans put forward by the Foundation was to keep the rear side of the Gallery white, ie the part facing west on the banks of the river Spree because it was always painted white in the life of the GDR so that anyone who managed to get over the Wall would be easily visible against the white backdrop. The reasoning put forward by the Berlin Wall Foundation was that the Gallery being a Historic Monument meant the rules had to be strictly adhered to. The Foundation was prepared to pay 30,000 Euros yearly for this.

As the Historic Monument Laws have been bent or ignored many times with regard to the East Side Gallery this argument doesn't hold. The East Side Gallery is a unique monument and has to be treated as such. A unique situation requires a unique solution.

Berlin Wall Foundation

A white wall anywhere is like a magnet to graffiti artists and it was obvious to most that keeping this side of the Wall white was going to be very costly and a complete waste of funds. Recent comments by the Foundation indicate that there may have been a sensible rethink on this.

On 1st November 2018 it was official; the Foundation was given full control over the future of the East Side Gallery. The Berlin Senate has made 250.000 Euros a year available to them for looking after the Gallery and its surroundings. I somehow suspect that it is not generally known that it wasn't only the East Side Gallery which was handed over to the Foundation they were also given complete control of what remains of the green space behind the Gallery. This is the area on banks of the river Spree which is currently used as a recreation area and at the moment, open to all.

Contractually the Foundation is required to hold regular 'Round Table' meetings so that interested parties can have their say on what happens with the Gallery. The 'Round Table' members do not however have any legal status and are not able to prevent decisions being made by the Foundation with which they don't agree.

Some of the East Side Gallery artists expressed the hope that since the Gallery is now in the care of the Berlin Wall Foundation they will all be treated equally. Regrettably one year on there is no sign that this has happened.

The artists were never contacted by the Foundation either shortly before or after becoming the official custodians. You would think that basic politeness alone would ensure that all the artists were contacted. It would seem therefore that the artists are to have no say in the future development of a Gallery which they co-created; their input isn't being sought and they have not been invited to take part in any decision making.

Think bigger

You wonder why in 28 years an East Side Gallery Foundation was never established? Also, in all that time there wasn't even a simple sign erected at each end of the Gallery with the most basic information such as who created it or its location in the former East Berlin. The argument of cost is a response of avoidance. The lack of funding could have been solved in several ways such as the setting up of a legal body which could receive donations. If only 50% of the many thousands of tourists who flock there each year donated 1 Euro a fund for the ongoing maintenance of the Gallery would quickly be established.

The extent of the worldwide significance of the East Side Gallery was never recognized by the Berlin authorities. For years it suffered from disrespect, neglect and abuse. It never received the recognition and praise it deserved.

What the East Side Gallery lacked after its completion were people with vision, big thinkers who could have promoted the Gallery in a respectful, positive way. People who would have ensured that the Historic Monument status was strictly adhered to irrespective of who tried to override it and that basic information on the origin and history of the Gallery was made available onsite. It is regrettable that no such visionaries were involved in or responsible for the Gallery as the outcome of its fate could have been so very different.

Thirty years on

So here we are in 2019 thirty years after the Berlin Wall opened and part of the East Side Gallery is still standing despite the many efforts to have it removed to make way for financial gain for a few.

As you will have gathered, it hasn't been easy to secure what is left of the gallery because of people in powerful positions who have no interest in adhering to laws, democracy or the wants and needs of the people. That's true almost everywhere, not only in Berlin. It's really only down to people power that it hasn't been completely removed already.

If there was a positive aspect of the Wall being in place then it was because it made Berlin totally unattractive for Property Speculators. The perception that the Property Industry is synonymous with greed and corruption often proves to be an accurate one.

Many people from the West think they live in a free society but they are deluding themselves. The restrictions and surveillance in the West may be more subtle but they still exist. Granted we have freedom of movement in the sense that we can travel almost anywhere we want if we can afford to, something the citizens of the GDR couldn't do but many in the West fall for the propaganda put out by their governments and think it is the truth.

In 2019 these restrictions and loss of what we thought were freedoms are much more obvious to those who look beyond the surface. Years ago people were spied on secretly now it happens quite openly as anyone who uses the internet has a smart phone or 'smart' anything is open to surveillance. There is no privacy anywhere anymore when you have to use modern technology. Most governments and institutions push people into using this technology whether they want to or not. The reasons for that are obvious.

"The best way to take control over a people and control them utterly is to take a little of their freedom at a time, to erode rights by a thousand tiny and almost imperceptible reductions. In this way, the people will not see those rights and freedoms being removed until past the point at which these changes cannot be reversed."
Pat Miller

What was it all about?

So what was it all about? A group of people came together to contribute their part to the whole which became the East Side Gallery. It is that of course but it is much more. It is much bigger than the sum of its parts. At the time, immediately after the Wall opened, many people wanted to tear down every last bit of it. The Germans have a reputation for not facing up to their past (but they are not the only ones – look at the evils of the British Empire) and just sweeping everything under the carpet in the hope that everyone will forget about it.

This wasn't going to happen to the Wall. This big grey lump of concrete which loomed over all of us who were ever up close and personal with it wasn't going to be ignored. Even if you never got physically close to the Wall the effect it had on everyone was there, somewhere in the air, especially in Berlin.

The diversity of the East Side Gallery is one of its strengths. It was never the intention to have 1.3 km of paintings by well known artists or to repeat a certain style. It could be viewed as Street Art because anyone who wished to could paint there and become part of the East Side Gallery. However, unlike Street Art which is fleeting by nature, the gallery was an organised project the artists were under contract and the paintings were protected. It is because of the organised nature of the East Side Gallery that it and its canvas, the Wall, has survived for so long.

Street art is constantly changing while the paintings of the East Side Gallery, with few exceptions, have not changed. When we create something we put our energy, some of our essence into it. Our energy is constantly changing, so that re-creating something years later will not imbue it with exactly the same energy.

What was it all about?

When one of the East Side Gallery artists dies, as a few have done, is their painting going to be re-created again and again by someone else as has been the case so far? The original paintings radiated a tangible energy that was perceived by others, as this excerpt from my diary confirms.

Diary entry 22/23.5.90

I met Ingeborg Ruthe from the NBI. She said that the editors had understood or were aware that the images in the ESG were sending a message. I found that quite amazing. It has, in a way, let me see the extent to which I am involved and the power behind the individual images or perhaps the collective effect.

The East Side Gallery is a historical monument and with its physical presence gives a tangible insight into a period of our history but sometimes the naming of something defines it in a restrictive way. It is regrettable if the East Side Gallery is categorized as something that must remain the same forever just because that is how monuments are usually dealt with because it is a restrictive definition of something unique.

The East Side Gallery is an enormously important testimony of history and culture. But it's not a dead museum, and although we didn't have a detailed plan when the gallery was founded, we never intended to create a dead museum.

Christine MacLean
Scotland 2019

Christine MacLean

Christine MacLean

Photo: David Edes

The gratitude bit

No person is an island and all creative works are the result of combined efforts even if we are unaware of the sometimes subconscious input by others in the form of stimulation, inspiration, casual comments etc. This book is a consciously combined effort of several people.

My gratitude for their support goes to: Claudia Linde for her help with translations and for kindly sharing her invaluable knowledge of life in the East; Doris Schüller for the generous gift of her time and knowledge in editing the German translation; my brother Angus and sister-in-law Rita for their encouragement and practical support.

Very special thanks go to Janette Wolff and Patricia Campbell who in different ways helped me keep a roof over my head whilst researching and writing this book. Only those who have found themselves threatened with nowhere to stay, no safe, secure haven, or have literally been homeless can really appreciate what it feels like to be without somewhere to call home.

Special thanks go to my friend Morag Foster for her generous financial support, her excellent editorial skills, her continuous encouragement, her time and for just being a lovely friend.

I also wish to thank all the lovely friends I have been blessed with for their patience, help and encouragement.

Participating artists

Note: I have intentionally left the list of artists in its original form even though some of the countries no longer exist.

Kamel Alavi Persia/W. Berlin	Pal Gerber Hungary	Jeanett Kipka E. Berlin
Kani Alavi Persia/W. Berlin	Gabor Gerhes Hungary	Thomas Klingenstein W. Berlin
Kasra Alavi Persia/W. Berlin	Schamil Gjmajew USSR/E.Berlin	Christos Koutsouras Greece/W.Germany
Jim Avignon W. Berlin	Barbara Greul Aschanta W. Germany	Jacob Köhler W. Germany
Ines Bayer E. Berlin	Gruppe Ciccolina Greta Csatlos & David Line W.Berlin	Gerald Kriedner W. Germany
Willi Berger E. Germany	Gruppe Stellvertretende Durstende Hungary	Jolly Kunjappu India/W. Germany
Karina Bjerregaard Denmark	Roland Gützlaff W. Berlin	Susanne Kunjappu- Jellinek W.Berlin
Ignasi Blanch Spain/W. Berlin	Sandor Györffyä Hungary	Sabine Kunz E. Germany
Ingeborg Blumenthal W. Germany	Lotte Haubart Denmark	Christine Kühn W. Berlin
Lislott Blunier Switzerland/W. Germany	Gabriel Heimler France/W. Berlin	Gerhard Lahr E. Berlin
Brigida Böttcher E. Germany	Raik Hönemann E. Berlin	Carmen Leidner W. Berlin
M. Eliza Budzinski E. Berlin	Margaret Hunter Scotland/W. Berlin	Peter Lorenz W. Germany

Participating artists

Miriam Butterfly W. Berlin	Jens Hübner E. Berlin	Mary Mackey USA
Stephan Cacciatore W. Germany	Gabor Imre Hungary	Pierre-Paul Maillé Canada/W. Berlin
Teresa Casanueva Cuba/E. Germany	Indiano (Jürgen Große) W. Berlin	Yvonne Matzat W. Berlin
Kiddy Citny W. Berlin	Dr. Phil Narendra K. Jain India/W. Berlin	Kikue Miyatake Japan/USA
Jens-Helge Dahmen E. Berlin	Jay-one France/USA	Siegrid Müller-Holtz W. Berlin
Mirta Domacinovic Yugoslavia/W. Germany	Rainer Jehle W. Berlin	Klaus Niethardt E. Germany
Irena Dubrowskaya USSR	Ralf Jesse W. Germany	Thierry Noir France/W. Berlin
Hans-Peter Dürhager W. Germany	Carsten Jost E. Berlin	Cesar Olhagaray Chile/E. Berlin
Marc Engel E. Germany	Andreas Kämper E. Berlin	Andreas Paulun W. Berlin
Salvadore de Fazio USA	Lance Keller USA/W. Berlin	Peter Peinziger E. Berlin
Oliver Feind E. Germany	Kentaur (Laszlo Erkel) Hungary	Fulvio Pinna Italy/W. Berlin
Tomas Fey W. Berlin	Youngram Kim- Hohlfeld Korea/W. Berlin	Karin Porath W. Germany

Participating artists

Christoph Frank W. Germany	Birgit Kinder E. Berlin	Patrizio Porracchia Italy/W. Germany
Christine Fuchs W. Berlin	Günther Schäfer W. Germany/USA	Lutz Pottien-Seiring W. Berlin
Kim Prisu (Joaquim Borregana) Portugal/France	Rosemarie Schinzler W. Germany	Alexey Taranin USSR
Sandor Racmolnar Hungary	Slawa Schljachow Wjatsches USSR/E. Berlin	Theodor Cheslaw Tezhik USSR
Muriel Raoux France	Henry Schmidt E. Germany	Karsten Thoms W. Germany
George-Lutz Rauschebart W. Germany	Andre Secrit E. Berlin	VR (Herve Morlay) France
Ditmar Reiter W. Berlin	Michail Serebrjakow USSR	Dmitri Vrubel USSR
Catrin Resch E. Germany	Gabor Simon E. Berlin	Andy Weiss W. Berlin
Rodolfo Ricalo Cuba/E. Germany	Andrej Smolak Czechoslovakia	Karsten Wenzel E. Berlin
Ana Leonor Rodriques Portugal/W. Berlin	Bodo Sperling W. Germany	Dieter Wien W. Germany
Peter Russell Scotland	Ulrike Steglich E. Berlin	Ursula Wünsch E. Berlin
Santoni Austria	Petra Suntinger W. Berlin	Ulrike Zott E. Berlin
		Karin Vellmans W. Germany

Links

https://www.youtube.com/watch?v=wrZctaHcXOQ&feature=youtu.be
Christine MacLean - interview with Maga Navarette of Pressenza.com

http://www.berliner-mauer.de/east-side-gallery
Ralf Gründer, films about the Berlin Wall

www.mauerfotos-aus-ostberlin.de
Wall photos from East Berlin by Detlef Matthes

www.wall-streetgallery.de
Wall-StreetGallery, Peter Unsicker, artist, sculptor, author

www.berlineastsidegallery.berlin
www.christine-maclean.com
Christine MacLean's websites

Mühlenstrasse 1990